Chicago Cubs

YESTERDAY & TODAY ™

Saul Wisnia
Foreword by Ron Santo

WEST SIDE PUBLISHING

Saul Wisnia's writing has appeared in *Sports Illustrated, The Boston Herald, Boston Globe, Boston Magazine,* and numerous other publications. A former sports and feature correspondent for *The Washington Post*, he authored *Baseball's Prime-Time Stars,* coauthored *Babe Ruth: His Life and Times* and *Wit & Wisdom of Baseball,* and was a contributing writer on books including *The Golden Age of Baseball, Best of Baseball, The Michael Jordan Scrapbook,* and *Treasury of Baseball.* He is currently senior publications editor at Dana-Farber Cancer Institute in Boston.

Ron Santo's name is synonymous with Chicago Cubs baseball. In his 14 seasons as the team's third baseman, he was a nine-time All-Star and five-time Gold Glove winner. In 2003, he became only the third player in franchise history to have his uniform number retired. He now provides color commentary for the team's radio broadcasts and acts as the celebrity chairman for the Juvenile Diabetes Research Foundation's Ron Santo Walk to Cure Diabetes.

Editorial consulting by Stuart Shea

Facts verified by Ken Samelson

Special thanks to collectors Art Ahrens; Mark Braun of the Old Timers' Baseball Association of Chicago; George Castle; Steve Gold of Au Sports Memorabilia, Inc.; Richard Johnson of the Sports Museum of New England; SAD Memorabilia.

ISBN-13: 978-1-4127-1503-4
ISBN-10: 1-4127-1503-2

Manufactured in China.

8 7 6 5 4 3 2 1

Library of Congress Control Number: 2007937672

The Chicago Cubs stand for the National Anthem at Wrigley Field before Game 3 of the National League Division Series on October 6, 2007.

Contents

1886 White Stockings   Page 20

Mordecai Brown   Page 32

1932 Cubs   Page 69

College of Coaches   Page 96

Billy Williams   Page 110

Greg Maddux   Page 144

Foreword

I've loved baseball for as long as I can remember. I have a picture from when I was 2 years old and my dad first put a real glove on my hand, and that's when it all started. When I was growing up in Seattle, Washington, we lived in a duplex. There was an old garage with no doors, and my stepbrother would pitch to me from about 30 feet away with a tennis ball. The only way I could get any base hits or drive in any runs was to hit line drives out of the garage; if I hit the ceiling I was out. We'd play that game all day long. When I was 7 or 8, I joined Little League as a shortstop and pitcher. By the time I was 12, I was an All-Star in the Pony League. The game came easy, but I always strived to do better.

Ron Santo

They didn't allow freshman to play varsity at Franklin High School, but a player got hurt so they brought me up to play third base. I played varsity basketball and football, too. But baseball was always my first love. I just couldn't get enough of the game. I lived two blocks from Sick's Stadium, where the Seattle Rainiers of the Pacific Coast League played. My freshman year I got a job on the stadium grounds crew, so I was there all during the summer. Later I became a bat boy, and then my senior year I became the clubhouse boy. Seattle was then a Triple-A affiliate of the Cincinnati Reds, and Vada Pinson was on the team. He could really fly, and any time he slid and got his pants dirty he'd want to change them. I just knew he was going to get to the big leagues.

My senior year I beat out 60 kids from the state of Washington, and I went to New York to play for the United States All-Stars against the New York All-Stars. I got two hits in the ball game, and from that point on the scouts were watching me. My stepfather and I made arrangements with each of the 16 major-league teams to come to town and negotiate contracts. A lot of teams made higher offers than the Cubs, but I always watched the "Game of the Week" on TV—and there was something about Wrigley Field that I loved. Ernie Banks was also something special, so at age 18, before the '59 season, I signed a Double-A contract with the Cubs. One year and two months later, I was in the big leagues playing alongside Ernie and against Vada Pinson. So I guess I made the right decision.

My first game in the majors was on June 26, 1960, at Pittsburgh's old Forbes Field. It was my first time ever in a big-league ballpark. In those days there were only 400 big-league ballplayers, so when a rookie took somebody's job, he had to prove himself. Ernie was the only guy who really talked to me, and he was everything I thought he would be and more. He was such a beautiful person, and what a great ballplayer. That first game I was hitting sixth against Vernon Law of the Pirates, and on my first time up I got a curve ball that backed me off the plate. Smoky Burgess was catching, and when he threw the ball back he said, "That's a major-league curveball, kid." I got nervous, but eventually I got a base hit up the middle and went 3-for-7 with 5 RBIs and we won a doubleheader.

Billy Williams had played with me in Double-A ball, and he came up in '61. To this day, Billy and I have played in more games as teammates than any two major-league ballplayers. He and Ernie were and are like family to me. Our wives have always gotten along great, too. It was that way with the whole Cubs ball club. It was just a great time to play; three guys on my team—Ernie, Billy, and Fergie Jenkins—became Hall of Famers. I was lucky enough to play on nine All-Star teams with hitters such as Aaron, Mays, and McCovey and pitchers such as Drysdale, Koufax, and Gibson. I feel it was the best era in baseball history, with the most talent. There is talent today, don't get me wrong, but that was the best. That was when 500 home runs, or even 300 or 400, really meant something.

I've spent the majority of my life in Chicago, and I feel like it is—no, there is no doubt about it—it is my home. There is an electricity you feel at certain ballparks, and I've always felt it at Wrigley Field. I was born and raised to play day ball, and the fans here are what the game is all about: Win or lose, they always show up. Cub fans never lose their allegiance, and there's a lot of tradition. They pass it on to their kids, and their kids after that. It's that kind of relationship; anywhere you go, in any city today, you're going to find Cub fans. They're the best I've ever been around, and I really enjoyed playing for them and then broadcasting for them the past 18 years. I'm as much a fan as they are. In fact, I feel I give *them* the opportunity to let everything out, because I do. That's how much they—and the Cubs— mean to me.

7

CHAPTER ONE

THE BEGINNING: 1876–1901

CHARTER MEMBERS OF the National League, the Cubs—then known as the White Stockings—were the circuit's first pennant winners in 1876 and its first "dynasty" with five more championships between 1880 and 1886. Led by venerable player-manager Cap Anson, with help from stars including "King" Kelly, Larry Corcoran, John Clarkson, and Jimmy Ryan, they thrilled fans in what was for many years the league's preeminent city.

Left: The 1876 White Stockings, champions in the maiden season of the National League, were heralded in numerous illustrations like this one—a precursor to today's glossy posters and magazines. *Right:* The second West Side Grounds (or Park), a wooden facility built in 1894, was home to four NL championship teams and the 1907 and 1908 World Series winners. As the Cubs excelled, more and more private boxes were built atop its grandstands.

Out of the Ashes Rises a New League—and a New Champion

In the days and weeks after October 1871, the last thing on the minds of most Chicagoans was baseball. The Great Fire that swept through town October 8–10 brought the city to a virtual standstill, and its path of destruction included the ballpark and equipment belonging to Chicago's premier team: the White Stockings. Although Chicago's entrant in the National Association of Professional Base Ball Players—the first acknowledged pro league—got through the waning days of the '71 season with road games and borrowed uniforms, they were disbanded after that campaign. There would be little time for America's pastime during the next few long years of rebuilding the region.

One man helping bring the city back to life was William A. Hulbert.

Described by one biographer as a "pitiless coal baron," White Stockings owner William A. Hulbert was responsible for both establishing the profitable National League and shifting baseball's power structure from players to owners.

A successful grain and coal merchant, he saw the potential for baseball's future success in a revived Chicago. The White Stockings were back in the National Association by '75, but they struggled to stay financially afloat. Hulbert, already a minority shareholder in the team, agreed to take over as its president in June. He knew his club was not alone in its troubles; the Association as a whole was floundering for a variety of reasons. Drunkenness, gambling, and even game-fixing were widespread problems among both players and fans, and team schedules were loosely set and even more loosely adhered to as the summers wore on.

A lack of competitive balance did not help matters. Boston's Red Stockings were cruising to their fourth-consecutive league pennant with a 71–8 record behind star pitcher Albert Goodwill "A. G." Spalding, and many clubs in the 13-team circuit felt they had no chance against this juggernaut. Sagging attendance suggested their fans didn't either. Due to a lack of resources, drive, or both, players routinely jumped from one team to another for higher contracts, often in midseason.

Like any good businessman, Hulbert saw a solution. He believed if clubs were in the

The popularity of players such as pitcher Jim McCormick, a 31-game winner for the champion White Stockings in 1886, was heightened by their inclusion along with other athletes on baseball's earliest commercial "trade cards." By the mid-1880s, several tobacco companies were inserting cards into packs of their products and distributing them nationally.

hands of savvy owners who could rein in irresponsible players and run a cleaner, more balanced league with tougher rules, stricter contracts, and set scheduling, profits would follow. Setting a goal of having Chicago become the class of a revamped circuit, Hulbert secretly went after the top performer in the National Association. Appealing to A. G. Spalding's competitive nature, he convinced the Rockford, Illinois, native that returning home and helping the White Stockings topple Boston from its perch would be the most fulfilling chapter of the hurler's career. Without revealing anything to the public, Spalding agreed to play for Chicago in 1876, as well as captain (manage) the team, for a tidy sum of $2,000 and 25 percent of the gate receipts.

Once on board, Spalding quietly went to work on his comrades. Soon he had enticed fellow Boston standouts Jim "Deacon" White (catcher), Cal McVey (first base), and Ross Barnes (second base) to join him, along with Philadelphia star Cap Anson. When word finally broke of the scheme, other National Association owners attempted to thwart it. Expecting this, Hulbert merely called their bluff by threatening to form his own league, then he did just that when the Association folded. The National League (NL) was formed on February 2, 1876, in New York's Grand Central Hotel, and it included eight teams (Boston, Hartford, New York, Philadelphia, Chicago, Louisville, Cincinnati, and St. Louis), all in cities of 75,000 or more. The owners and players were willing to adhere to Hulbert's rules: strict schedules, no gambling, and no alcohol in the ballparks. Fines would be levied for any infractions.

On April 25, 1876, the White Stockings played their inaugural National League game, a 4–0 road win over the Louisville Grays. Albert Spalding hurled the shutout, had three hits, and then two days later blanked the Grays again. Chicago was off and running to the circuit's first championship. Today, the descendants of that club (now called the Cubs) are still suiting up as the last remaining original NL franchise playing in its city of origin.

Even in the days when pitchers routinely finished what they started, Spalding stood out. The Hall of Famer had 281 complete games in 327 career starts, and he pitched 528⅔ innings for the White Stockings in 1876—all but 63⅓ of the club's total played. His .796 lifetime winning percentage plus his standing as baseball's greatest ambassador sealed his 1939 Cooperstown selection.

ALBERT GOODWILL SPALDING
ORGANIZATIONAL GENIUS OF BASEBALL'S PIONEER DAYS. STAR PITCHER OF FOREST CITY CLUB IN LATE 1860's, 4-YEAR CHAMPION BOSTONS 1871-1875 AND MANAGER-PITCHER OF CHAMPION CHICAGOS IN NATIONAL LEAGUE'S FIRST YEAR. CHICAGO PRESIDENT FOR 10 YEARS. ORGANIZER OF BASEBALL'S FIRST ROUND-THE-WORLD TOUR IN 1888.

Speedy backup outfielder Billy Sunday was a nondrinker on a club of carousers. Sunday's clean living made him a favorite of the growing temperance movement and straight-laced Albert Spalding. Sunday began his second career as a Christian speaker while still with the team. After quitting baseball in 1891, he became a heralded and influential evangelist.

THE NAME GAME: WHITE STOCKINGS...COLTS...ORPHANS?

Although the Cubs are the only original National League team still playing in its city of origin, the ballclub—like many during the 1876–1901 period—underwent a series of name changes in its formative years. In those days, a team was often named for its hometown, its owner, or its uniform components. Sometimes new nicknames were the brainchild of sportswriters, and some teams even had different newspapers or fans calling them different things at the same time.

For the record, the Cubs were officially known as the White Stockings (or Whites) when the NL was formed in 1876, and they kept this name through their first 14 seasons. (This should not be confused with the American League's White Sox, who would start play in 1900.) Next they became the Colts (1890–1902), and finally, in 1902, the Cubs. Several other nicknames such as Rainmakers and Rough Riders never fully caught on, and the funniest had to be a moniker many fans used for several years after longtime manager Cap Anson's 1898 firing: the Orphans.

Diamonds from Dumps: Chicago's First Ballpark Revival

Chicago played its home games during the National League's inaugural season of 1876 in a modest wooden ballpark; it was called the 23rd Street Grounds so fans would know where to find it. Described by one source as "a ramshackle facility," it stood out in no memorable way from the NL's other humble structures. The White Stockings became champions despite this uninspiring abode, but when they leased a new ballpark on Randolph Street and Michigan Avenue for the 1879 campaign, conditions went from mediocre to awful. Lake Front Park had most recently served as a dump for the city's Great Fire of '71, and players had to endure a bumpy infield strewn with rocks and debris. Once again, however, the team overshadowed its dismal dwelling with three straight pennants from 1880 to 1882.

The next year, with Chicago contending yet again, owner Al Spalding apparently felt the team and its fans were finally deserving of something better. Lake Front Park was completely remodeled during 1883 into a grand facility befitting a champion, at a cost of $10,000. Its seating capacity was expanded from 3,000 to 10,000, including both a standing-room section and 18 skyboxes above the third-base stands. The skyboxes, a new innovation, came equipped with armchairs and curtains. Spalding's private box even featured a telephone (still a novelty) and a Chinese gong for getting the attention of manager Cap Anson. A ballpark staff of 41 included 8 musicians who played in a pagoda over the main entrance.

The majority of seats were elevated to maximize fan viewing, but the ballpark had one major shortcoming: its dimensions. Though it featured the NL's largest seating capacity, its outfield distances were the shortest in big-league history: just 180 feet to left field, 280–300 feet to center, and 196 feet to right. In 1884 the White Stockings took advantage of their cozy confines by out-homering their NL rivals 142–83, but when the league set a 210-foot minimum for outfield fences after that season, the Lake Front bashing stopped. Spalding's club would be moving again.

DEDICATION
—OF THE—
New Chicago Base Ball Park,
COR. CONGRESS AND LOOMIS STS.,
SATURDAY, JUNE 6th., 3:40 P.M.
ST. LOUIS VS. CHICAGO.

After leaving Lake Front Park, the White Stockings moved to the first West Side Grounds in 1885. It was located two miles west of downtown Chicago and featured modern restroom facilities, private boxes, a covered area in the outfield to park carriages, and terra-cotta paint adorning the woodwork. The team earned NL championships their first two seasons there.

Early Glory:
6 Pennants in 11 Years

Given the team's long recent World Series drought, it's hard to imagine that the Cubs were ever considered baseball's grandest champions. But after debuting with a first-place finish in the National League's inaugural season of 1876, Chicago went on to claim additional pennants in 1880, '81, '82, '85, and '86 and supplant the Boston Nationals as baseball's dominant team.

Led by the nucleus of Albert Spalding, Cap Anson, Deacon White, Cal McVey, and Ross Barnes, the White Stockings finished their maiden NL campaign with a 52–14 record, good for a six-game advantage over runners-up St. Louis and Hartford in the eight-team league. Spalding, serving as captain (manager) and ace pitcher, led the NL in wins with 47. Second baseman Barnes topped all league hitters in batting average (.429), while third sacker Anson checked in at .356. Spalding's retirement from the pitching ranks due to injury the next season and Barnes's sharp decline at the plate prompted three years of fourth- or fifth-place finishes, but Chicago was back on top in 1880 at 67–17, good for a scintillating .798 winning percentage.

Anson was serving as manager and first baseman, and with new stars including Mike "King" Kelly and George Gore on board, he had a dynastic lineup of imposing physical specimens (many more than 6 feet tall) capable of intimidating opponents. Pitchers Larry Corcoran and Fred Goldsmith backed this giant attack by winning at least 21 games apiece for four straight years, and when they faltered in 1885, John Clarkson and Jim McCormick stepped in as a dynamic hurling duo. By the end of the '86 season, Anson had claimed five pennants in eight years at the helm, and his team enjoyed both a loyal fan following and a beautiful ballpark. The future promised more of the same.

Clean-cut looks can be deceiving. Like many great teams, the White Stockings of 1880–86 liked to have fun away from the ballpark. The lineup that produced five pennants in eight years also produced countless empty beer glasses and late-night escapades, with King Kelly (upper left) considered the biggest culprit.

A. G. Spalding: Pitcher to President

Despite just one full season among the club's playing ranks, Al Spalding had an impact on the team and game that is still felt 125 years after his last contest. The motto of Chicago's first star was "Everything is possible to him who dares," and certainly few in baseball history dared or accomplished more.

Albert Goodwill Spalding (known as "Al" or "A. G.") was born in Byron, Illinois, but during the early 1870s he found fame pitching for the Boston Red Stockings. Lured back to his home state by Chicago owner William A. Hulbert for the National League's inaugural season of 1876, the 6'1" right-hander helped Hulbert amass a powerhouse club. With a 47–12 record and 1.75 ERA, he led the team to the first-ever NL pennant. He played first base and outfield when not pitching, hit .312, and served as captain (manager).

The '76 title cemented Spalding's status as baseball's top star, but at the start of the 1877 season he hurt his arm. Shockingly, his pitching career was over at age 26, leaving him the legacy of a 253–65 career record that would earn him Hall of Fame induction. He gutted it out for 60 games as an infielder during the summer of '77, but after a one-game cameo the next spring he was done as a player.

Turning to the business end of the game, Spalding became Chicago's club secretary (equivalent to today's general manager) and helped assemble another championship team. Elected president of the White Stockings upon Hulbert's 1882 death, he held the position for a decade and did his part to stamp out a rival Player's League in 1890. He even led a contingent of stars from his and other NL clubs on an around-the-world tour, introducing America's pastime to such distant locales as Egypt, Italy, and Australia. His attempt to bring night baseball to Chicago was less successful, but that was one of the few "strikeouts" in Spalding's illustrious career.

By the early 20th century, Spalding had been out of baseball as a player for more than a quarter century, but he was still one of the game's most respected figures—and still a fan of his beloved Chicago club.

SPALDING KEEPS ON PITCHING

Long after his 1878 retirement from playing, Albert Spalding was still pitching baseballs—and plenty else. Two years earlier, he and his brother had opened a "sports emporium" where they sold baseball and other sporting merchandise.

The result was a huge success. Spalding's status as a star athlete made him a celebrity in the business world. By 1901, Spalding Sporting Goods had 14 stores (including the one above) making and selling products. The company supplied the National League with all its official baseballs, produced the league's first rule book, and turned out an annual *Baseball Guide* that became the game's gold standard publication.

Ageless Cap Anson: Chicago's "Mr. Baseball"

Conditioning being what it was in the 19th century and with far fewer medical remedies available for major injuries, it's no surprise that many early big-leaguers had their careers fizzle at around age 30. Several top Chicago players were among them, but teetotaler Cap Anson defied this standard by staying in superb shape and lasting 22 years in a White Stockings uniform—homering twice on his final afternoon in the majors at the ripe age of 45.

Born in a log cabin on the Iowa frontier, Adrian Constantine Anson was named after two Michigan towns his father had lived in as a child. In time, however, fans granted him a series of nicknames—the most popular of which honored his status as captain (manager) of the Chicago club. A catcher in the minors, the right-handed batter later starred at third with the Philadelphia Athletics of the National Association before White Stockings owner William A. Hulbert persuaded him to join his squad in 1876.

During the 22 seasons to come, the final 19 as Chicago's player-manager, Anson settled in at first base and collected two batting titles, 2,076 RBI, and 3,418 hits (the first big-leaguer to reach 3,000). A keen eye for talent served him well as a leader, as did his status as the NL's biggest player at 6′1″, 220 pounds. He didn't mind getting physical to make a point, and his style was effective: His five NL championships and 1,283 victories are both still team records, and his .578 lifetime winning percentage ranks him among baseball's all-time best skippers.

Anson was very popular among fans, teammates, and opponents despite bucking convention as a fitness buff and healthy eater who didn't smoke or drink. His players might not have enjoyed the strict daily workouts he required, but when someone lasts 27 pro seasons (including his Philadelphia years) and bats .335 at age 43, people tend to respect the approach. And while Cap's disdain for black ballplayers is truly unconscionable, the Hall of Famer's status as one of the best players of the pre-1900 era—if not *the* best—is secure.

The 1876 White Stockings did not originate the term "Chicagoed"—coined a few years earlier as a descriptor for shutouts by any club—but they took the phrase to new heights by routinely trouncing the opposition.

In an era when racism permeated much of professional baseball, Anson was one of the worst offenders. He wrote openly of his disdain for black players in his 1900 autobiography, and on the field he backed up his words by taunting or refusing to play against nonwhite athletes.

THIS EARLY WOODCUT DECLARES THE CHICAGO WHITE STOCKINGS "U.S." CHAMPIONS FOLLOWING THEIR 1876 PENNANT-WINNING SEASON.

NED WILLIAMSON THRIVED IN LAKE FRONT PARK, WITH ITS SIX-FOOT-HIGH FENCE IN LEFT JUST 180 FEET FROM HOME PLATE. HE HIT 27 HOME RUNS IN 1884, A RECORD THAT STOOD FOR 35 YEARS.

A CENTURY BEFORE MLB.COM, THIS GUIDE WAS CONSIDERED THE GAME'S GOLD STANDARD STATISTICAL SOURCE—AS MUCH FOR THE REVERED NAME ADORNING IT AS FOR ITS CONTENT.

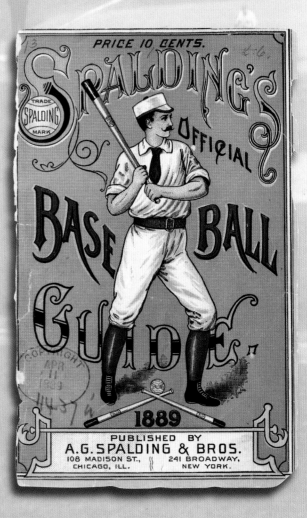

Ross Barnes goes 6-for-6 for Chicago in lopsided win

CHICAGO, July 27, 1876—White Stockings second baseman Ross Barnes had a perfect day at the plate today with a 6-for-6 effort in Chicago's 17–3 victory over the visiting Cincinnati Reds at the 23rd Street Grounds.

Barnes's output, which included a double and triple, marked the third time in the past week that a Chicago player collected six hits. The red-hot White Stockings have now won nine straight games, and their 34–7 record gives them a six-game lead over second-place Hartford in the National League. Ross, you may recall, hit the first home run in league annals on May 2—also against Cincinnati.

HULBERT'S ALL-BUSINESS ATTITUDE COULD BE SUMMED UP IN A SINGLE QUOTE: "IT IS RIDICULOUS TO PAY BALLPLAYERS $2,000 A YEAR, ESPECIALLY WHEN THE $800 BOYS OFTEN DO JUST AS WELL." HE RECEIVED COOPERSTOWN RECOGNITION IN 1995.

WILLIAM AMBROSE HULBERT

WAVY-HAIRED, SILVER TONGUED EXECUTIVE AND ENERGETIC, INFLUENTIAL LEADER. WHILE PART-OWNER OF CHICAGO NATIONAL ASSOCIATION TEAM, WAS INSTRUMENTAL IN FOUNDING NATIONAL LEAGUE IN 1876. ELECTED N.L. PRESIDENT LATER THAT YEAR AND IS CREDITED WITH ESTABLISHING RESPECTABILITY, INTEGRITY AND SOUND FOUNDATION FOR NEW LEAGUE WITH HIS RELENTLESS OPPOSITION TO BETTING, ROWDINESS, AND OTHER PREVALENT ABUSES WHICH WERE THREATENING THE SPORT

THE EARLIEST BASEBALL CARDS GAVE MANY FANS THEIR FIRST CHANCE TO SEE THEIR HEROES UP CLOSE. THIS CARD DEPICTS WHITE STOCKINGS RIGHT-HANDER MARK BALDWIN, WHO WENT 18-17 AS AN 1887 ROOKIE.

IN ADDITION TO PROMOTING BASEBALL NATIONALLY, ALBERT SPALDING OCCASIONALLY TOOK HIS SHOW ABROAD, INCLUDING A SIX-MONTH "WORLD TOUR" IN 1888-89 ON WHICH HIS CHICAGO CLUB AND OTHER ALL-STARS SUITED UP AMID THE PYRAMIDS OF EGYPT.

THE 1892 COLTS WENT 70-76 FOR THE SEASON AND FINISHED SEVENTH IN THE NATIONAL LEAGUE.

Great Arms of Old: Larry Corcoran and John Clarkson

A photographer's studio captured the pitching motion of John Clarkson, who produced a league-leading 308 strike-outs in 1885 using a then-unique overhand fastball. Despite his success, he was plagued by a fragile ego. "Scold him, find fault with him, and he could not pitch at all," Cap Anson recalled. "Praise him, and he was unbeatable."

Pitchers started (and completed) nearly all their team's games during pro baseball's earliest years, but in 1879 player-manager Cap Anson began testing the concept of a "rotation" in which two hurlers traded off starts to save arm strength. The experiment was a success, and the White Stockings soon rode to five National League pennants in seven years thanks largely to "No. 1" right-handers Larry Corcoran and John Clarkson.

First up was Corcoran, who joined Chicago in 1880. Despite his slight stature (5'3", 120 pounds), he had a blazing fastball and went 43–14 with a 1.95 ERA for the NL champs while aided admirably by No. 2 man Fred Goldsmith (21–3). Corcoran is credited by most historians as the first pitcher to devise a set of signals with his catcher, and the strategy clearly worked: Among the rookie's five shutouts that season was a no-hitter against Boston on August 19, the first ever by a Chicago pitcher.

The rotation concept took full hold in '81, and Corcoran went 31–14 to help Chicago to its second straight title. In 1882 he was 27–12 with a 1.95 ERA and threw a second no-hitter for the three-peaters, and he even hit a grand slam—another first in club annals. Two years later he recorded yet another no-hitter; only Nolan Ryan and Sandy Koufax would ever top his total of three.

Corcoran had 170 wins in just five seasons entering 1885, but early that year a "lame arm" prompted his retirement. As if on schedule, a new No. 1 starter emerged: John Clarkson. With the season expanded to 110-plus games, Clarkson—one of the majors' early overhand hurlers—handled the bulk of them and topped the league in wins (53–16) as Chicago returned to first place. Jim McCormick, Jocko Flynn, and Mark Baldwin spelled him more during 1886–87. But at 35–17 and 38–21 those seasons, Clarkson still led the NL in victories in '87. He also joined Corcoran in the no-hit ranks with a gem at Providence in 1885. But before the '88 season, he was sold to his hometown Boston Nationals for a then-staggering $10,000. There he eventually reached 328 wins and the Hall of Fame. Sadly, both pitching greats died young: Clarkson of Bright's disease at age 47, Corcoran of pneumonia at 32.

JOHN GIBSON CLARKSON
WORCESTER, N.L. 1882
CHICAGO, N.L. 1884-87
BOSTON, N.L. 1888-92
CLEVELAND, N.L. 1892-94
PITCHED 4 TO 0 NO-HIT GAME AGAINST
PROVIDENCE IN 1885. WON 328 LOST 175
PCT. 652 LED LEAGUE WITH 53 VICTORIES
IN 1885 (INCLUDING 10 SHUTOUTS) 38 IN
1887, 49 IN 1888 AND 49 IN 1889. HAD
2013 STRIKEOUTS IN 4514 INNINGS.

Clarkson's likeness was cast in bronze at Cooperstown in 1963, but his right arm meant gold back in 1888—when he was reunited with catcher King Kelly on the Boston Nationals. Kelly had been sold to Boston the year before, and the record $10,000 price tag paid for each earned the duo a logical nickname: "The $20,000 Battery."

"King" Kelly, the People's Choice

Part slugger, part showman, all competitor, Michael James "King" Kelly is usually considered by historians to be baseball's first true superstar. A worthy predecessor to Babe Ruth in his ability to generate excitement on the field and newspaper headlines off it, the catcher-outfielder delighted fans with his speed, skill, and a blatant disregard for rules.

Born—fittingly—on New Year's Eve to Irish immigrants, Kelly was an orphan by age 13 and an amateur baseball standout just a few years later. The New Jersey native reached the majors with Cincinnati in 1887, and he was third in hitting with a .348 mark in '79. He also showed speed with 12 triples, and when he was released along with his entire underachieving team, the White Stockings quickly acquired Kelly's services.

Then the biggest city in the National League, Chicago was the perfect locale for Kelly's brash talent to burst forth, just as New York City would be for Ruth 40 years later. Teammate Cap Anson had more power, but Kelly could work pitchers ragged with foul balls and then slap hits into the gaps. He also had a fierce desire to win, often going above the (baseball) law to do so. One of his favorite tricks—provided the umpire wasn't looking—was to cut across the diamond and skip second base in going from first to third. He is credited with perfecting the take-out slide at second to break up double plays and, on defense, was known to trip baserunners and hide extra balls in the grass for when he needed them.

Fans loved the handsome performer with the handlebar mustache and flashy wardrobe, especially when Kelly supported his outrageous behavior with strong play. He helped Chicago to five NL pennants, won batting titles in 1884 (.354) and '86 (.388), and topped the circuit in runs scored each season from 1884 to '86. The future Hall of Famer became known as the "King of Baseball," but his passion for saloons and women didn't sit well with teetotaler White Stockings owner Al Spalding, who sold his biggest box-office attraction to Boston for $10,000 after the championship '86 season. The move made national headlines, proved a dud for Spalding, and outraged Chicagoans: As the photos of Kelly adorning countless saloon walls gathered dust, their team wouldn't finish first again for 20 years.

King Kelly was a quick thinker on the field, as well as mischievous. He once supposedly made a twisting, leaping grab of a deep fly ball to end a game, then revealed in the dugout that he actually hadn't caught the ball at all—or even knew where it had landed.

MIKE J. (KING) KELLY
COLORFUL PLAYER AND AUDACIOUS BASE-RUNNER. IN 1887 FOR BOSTON HE HIT .394 AND STOLE 84 BASES. HIS SALE FOR $10,000 WAS ONE OF THE BIGGEST DEALS OF BASEBALL'S EARLY HISTORY.

Cooperstown recognized Mike Kelly's talents as a ballplayer with induction in 1945, more than 50 years after his untimely death from pneumonia at age 36. The man who once commanded baseball's top salary had died penniless, the result of extravagant living—and drinking. Upon his induction, Hall of Fame officials couldn't even find Kelly's daughter to invite her to the ceremony.

Chicago's Lost World Championship Games

It's only fitting, Cubs fans can lament, that in addition to setting a record for World Series futility, their team appeared in two additional postseason showdowns that today are not even deemed authentic. Major League Baseball cites the Boston-Pittsburgh battle of 1903 as the first "official" World Series, but during the 1880s, the pennant-winning White Stockings twice squared off in playoffs then referred to as world championships.

The first, in 1885, pitted Chicago's National League titlists against the American Association champion St. Louis Browns. Although the NL had established itself as baseball's top circuit, smaller leagues such as the American Association wanted to prove their worth. The Browns, predecessors of the modern-day Cardinals, challenged the White Stockings to a best-of-12 series. The opener ended in a 5–5 tie when darkness halted play at Chicago's West Side Grounds, and the White Stockings took the second contest in St. Louis by forfeit when Browns manager Charles Comiskey pulled his team off the field in the sixth inning to protest the calls of umpire David Sullivan (who needed police protection to escape the angry fans).

St. Louis rebounded to win Games 3 and 4, but attendance dropped sharply when play shifted to neutral American Association sites for seven more scheduled contests. With Chicago up 3 games to 2, the teams decided to throw out the forfeit and play one winner-take-all finale in Cincinnati. St. Louis took the title with a 13–4 victory, but in the aftermath Chicago manager Cap Anson appealed that the forfeited win be restored. It was, leaving the series forever tied at 3–3–1 and setting in motion a rivalry that continues to this day.

The teams split a disappointing $1,000 in prize money for their efforts. After repeating as champs in their respective leagues, they met again for the 1886 championship. A best-of-seven format and $14,000 prize were the stakes this time, and Chicago lost in six games played before large, boisterous crowds. Today both series are considered by MLB to have been exhibitions, but at the time they certainly seemed real enough.

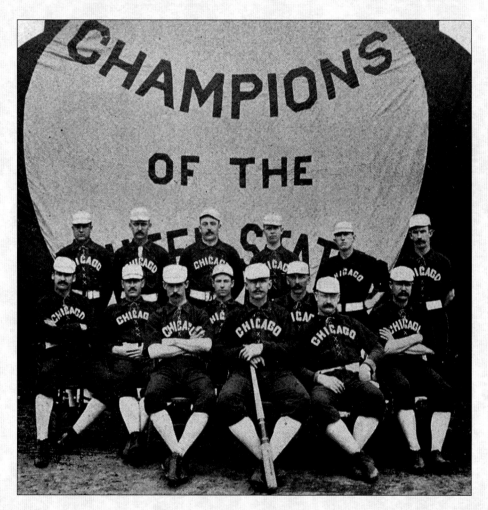

After capturing a second straight NL pennant, the 1886 White Stockings had a best-of-seven "world championship" rematch with the American Association's St. Louis Browns. Chicago lost the sixth and deciding game 4–3 in the tenth inning when John Clarkson's poor throw to nab St. Louis runner Curt Welch stealing home (some recalled it as a wild pitch) got past catcher King Kelly.

Jimmy Who?: Remembering a Forgotten Star

He lacked the firm leadership of Cap Anson and the flamboyant style of King Kelly, but Jimmy Ryan deserves to be included alongside those two stars when talk turns to Chicago's best 19th century ballplayers. His name itself is so plain that it can easily be forgotten, but anybody wanting to remember it need only glance at the team's all-time leader charts, where it appears quite high in several categories and alone at the top for triples with 142.

Ryan was born in Clinton, Massachusetts, during the Civil War. He played college baseball close to home at Holy Cross. Another product (along with other standouts such as Kelly and John Clarkson) of player-manager Anson's excellent scouting eye,

Virtually unknown today to all but diehard Cubs fans and baseball historians, Jimmy Ryan was a major star in his era. Upon his 1903 retirement, he ranked fourth all-time among major leaguers in doubles (451) and homers (118) and fifth in runs (1,642) and hits (2,502). His 356 assists as an outfielder remain an NL record.

the compact (5'9", 160 pounds) right-handed batter was brought to the White Stockings at the end of the 1885 season and started in their outfield for 14 of the next 15 years, with occasional sojourns to second, short, third, and even the pitcher's mound.

"Pony" was a model of consistency. Including his 1890 season with Chicago's entry in the renegade Player's League, he batted .300 or better 11 times (with a high of .361 in 1894), scored 82 runs or more for 13 straight campaigns, and recorded 25 or more steals on nine occasions. Ryan led the NL at least once in home runs, slugging, doubles, hits, on-base percentage, and total bases, and while never tops in triples, he collected ten or more nine times. He hit for the cycle twice (in 1888 and '91), and in the field he had excellent range and a terrific throwing arm.

Despite playing in fewer games, Ryan ranks alongside the top Cubs in triples (first), runs scored (1,409, second only to Anson), steals (369, third), hits (2,073, eighth), doubles (362, eighth), RBI (914, ninth), and batting average (.307, eleventh). He also went 6–1 with a 3.62 ERA in 24 games as a pitcher. While the newspaper columns and Web sites devoted to securing Hall of Fame recognition for Cubs great Ron Santo present good arguments, James Edward Ryan is just as deserving, even if most sportswriters and bloggers have never heard of him.

"Anson Is Out"

By the 1890s, Adrian "Cap" Anson had come to symbolize the past and present of Chicago's National League club. As a manager he was respected by his players, and as a teammate he routinely hit .330 or better. Even after dismantling the team following its '86 world championship loss to St. Louis, he had fielded competitive clubs.

Anson enjoyed an amicable relationship with team president Al Spalding—his old teammate—and he had signed a ten-year contract in 1888. When Spalding retired and named Jim Hart his successor in 1892, however, things got stickier. Hart and Anson did not get along; Hart saw Cap as a fossil left over from a different era, and Anson liked doing things his way. It was a classic impasse, but Hart had the power. All he needed was an excuse to use it.

As the new century neared, he got one. Anson turned 40 in '92, and while he often still hit at a strong clip, he was playing less and slipping defensively. In 1897, his average fell to .285, and with young teammates now growing tired of his style, he announced his retirement as a player. Although his Colts also slipped to a ninth-place finish, Cap's worst ever, Anson was looking forward to his 20th season as manager. Instead, Hart asked him to resign. Cap refused.

Then, on February 1, 1898, came the bombshell: Anson was fired, and former teammate Tom Burns was named the new manager. *The Sporting News*—the paper of record for baseball enthusiasts—blasted "Anson Is Out" across its front page, and Colts fans were left to ponder a future without the face of their franchise. For comparison's sake, it was akin to what it would have been like if the Orioles of the early 1990s had released an aging Cal Ripken; to many Chicagoans, it was as if their own father or brother had been kicked out of the family.

Anson kept very busy after his baseball career ended. He was an author, he was elected city clerk in Chicago from 1905 to 1907, and in 1908 he purchased and managed a semi-pro team, Anson's Colts.

Before he fell out of favor and was fired, Anson was among baseball's greatest and most marketable stars. Judging from the discarded bottles in this 1888 advertisement, he and New York Giants great Buck Ewing were likely through playing for the day.

A Day at the Ballpark, 1881

Although they dressed in bowler caps, suit coats, and ties, baseball fans (known as "cranks" or "bugs") during the game's pre-1900 era were not always the most dignified of patrons. A good number of these mostly middle-class men could be found gambling in the stands on the outcome of every pitch, then mixing things up with their fellow patrons when the action didn't go their way. The ballpark was not considered an appropriate place to take a young child or woman, and those in the latter group who did come could find themselves open to ridicule.

For a few nickels beyond their 50-cent admission (box seats might cost $1.00), fans going to Chicago's Lake Front Park in 1881 by foot or horse and buggy could enjoy sandwiches, soft drinks, and peanuts (hot dogs were not yet the rage). They had, however, challenges to contend with that went beyond the occasional inclement weather. The park's locale—beside the Illinois Central Railroad, with windy Lake Michigan just beyond it and dumps left over from the Great Fire of '71 next door—resulted in smoke from passing trains, sand from nearby beaches, and debris from the dumps all blowing in cranks' faces. Although this and other National League ballparks were then dry facilities—as opposed to parks in the American Association, which sold beer to patrons—fans at Lake Front undoubtedly found it easier to deal with the flying rubbish if they downed a few cold ones at a nearby saloon beforehand.

The team they cheered for was intoxicating in its own right. The White Stockings of 1881 were one of the greatest clubs in baseball history, with a powerful lineup featuring Cap Anson and Mike "King" Kelly, the most electric performer of his day. Kelly's magnetism on the basepaths and his strong hitting were appealing, of course, but he also engaged in an ongoing banter with fans unlike any player before. They delighted in his hook slides, laughed when he tripped an opposing ballplayer or otherwise bent the rules, and could even hope to walk down the street and share a beer with him after the game. They knew, of course, that the King always insisted on paying.

"Cranks" in the outfield seats cheer on their White Stockings at Lake Front Park, which by this point had already undergone its 1883 refurbishing. When he couldn't purchase the land where it stood and enlarge the facility due to a federal ordinance prohibiting the parcel's sale for a commercial venture, Al Spalding moved his club to West Side Grounds two years later.

VIEW LOOKING SOUTH.

CHAPTER TWO

WINDY CITY GLORY: 1902–1913

THE FIRST YEARS of the 20th century included the second dynastic stretch for the Colts/Cubs, a team that won four NL pennants and two World Series from 1906 to 1910. Legendary players who a century later still need no first-name introduction—Tinker, Evers, Chance, "Three Finger" Brown—lead the way. In 1906, the team turned in a regular-season performance for the ages: 116–36, which was the most victories ever by a team in the 154-game era. It has never been topped, even with eight more games now in the schedule.

Like many player-managers of the era, Frank Chance also coached third base. When he was at bat or on the bases, however, a teammate might handle the task. Here it's Johnny Evers on coaching duty, waving in his double-play partner during a game with archrival New York at a packed West Side Grounds.

The Cubs clawed their opponents at West Side Grounds in 1908, compiling a .610 home winning percentage. But they were even more ferocious on the road, where they went 52–25 (.675). They'd need every win in their thrilling pennant race with the Giants and Pirates.

Frank Selee's Contribution, Chicago's Greatest Teams

The 20th century dawned dismally for the Colts. They stumbled to a fifth-place finish in 1900 and then dropped to sixth (with a pitiful 53–86 record) a year later. Their glory years of the 1880s—when the club claimed five National League pennants in seven years—were receding further into the past. Nobody had stepped forward to fill the leadership void left by Cap Anson since his dismissal as player-manager in 1898. To make matters worse, five players from the club "jumped" across town to the Chicago White Sox of the upstart American League when it declared itself the second "major" league in '01. The AL's more lucrative contracts were too much for many NL athletes to resist.

Help was on the way, however. In 1902, Frank Selee took over as Colts manager from the forgettable Tom Loftus. Selee, a mild-mannered master strategist who had guided Boston's NL club to five pennants during the previous decade, made an immediate impact. He focused on developing young players, including Jimmy Slagle in left field, Johnny Kling at catcher, and Carl Lundgren in the pitching rotation. Kling's emergence enabled Selee to move his second-string catcher, Frank Chance, to first. The infield took further shape when young Joe Tinker took over at short. The final key piece in the puzzle came late in the year with the insertion of Johnny Evers at second base, and the first Tinker-to-Evers-to-Chance double play

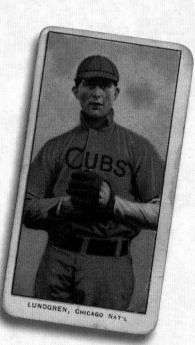

LUNDGREN, CHICAGO NAT'L

More than 24,000 fans endured the rain at West Side Grounds to see the Cubs and White Sox battle in Game 3 of their 1909 exhibition "City Series." The Sox won this wet encounter 2–1, but the Cubs prevailed in the annual showdown, four games to one.

Carl Lundgren was not as acclaimed as other Cubs starting pitchers in the early 1900s, but the Illinois native was a consistent winner—going 17–6 and 18–7 for the NL pennant winners of '06 and '07. His 1907 ERA of 1.17 is the ninth-lowest seasonal mark ever for a hurler throwing more than 200 innings.

WHITE SOX vs. CUBS
CITY CHAMPIONSHIP SERIES
Chicago, Oct. 10, '09 West Side Park.

The skies cleared for Cubs fans when Selee took over the club. Although the bald, short, sad-eyed skipper didn't look the part of a confident baseball man, he would turn the slumping club around immediately.

came against Cincinnati on September 15, 1902, at West Side Grounds. There would be many more.

Selee's moves brought the young club up to nearly .500 (at 68–69) in 1902. That season, the team earned the nickname of "Cubs," and the fans took to it immediately, though the squad would still officially be the Colts for three more years. The team took a second huge leap in 1903 with an 82–56 record and a third-place finish, then they moved up to 93–60 and second in '04. The latter year featured the emergence of Mordecai "Three Finger" Brown as the staff ace, a label he would carry for years to come. Chance was the club's lone .300 hitter, but stellar defense and pitching had become the team's calling cards. Another 90-win season followed in 1905, but for the second straight year Chicago finished 13 games behind the mighty New York Giants. The big addition to this campaign was another star pitcher, Ed Reulbach. The big loss was manager Selee, who retired due to tuberculosis on August 1.

Chance succeeded Selee, and thanks to his efforts and the groundwork laid by his predecessor, what followed was the greatest five-year stretch in Chicago's long National League history. Between 1906 and 1910, the Cubs compiled a 530–235 record—good for an incredible winning percentage of .693. They set records for most victories in a three-, four-, and five-year span, all of which stood long after teams began playing eight more games each season. They toppled two-time defending NL champ New York with a record 116 victories in 1906 (since

tied but never topped). After being upset by their crosstown rival White Sox in the World Series, they took the next step with two more pennants and a pair of World Series triumphs over Ty Cobb's Detroit Tigers in 1907 and 1908. Kling, Tinker, Evers, and player-manager Chance were key to the surge, as were pitchers Brown, Reulbach, Jack Pfiester, and Orval Overall. Other standouts emerged each season.

It took 110 wins from the Pittsburgh Pirates to end Chicago's three-year hold on the National League in 1909, but the Cubs still recorded 104 victories—a total they matched a year later when they took yet another NL crown before falling to the Philadelphia A's in the World Series. A slow decline was about to begin, but Cubs fans had enjoyed enough thrills to last them a while.

FINALLY, IT'S "CUBS"

Chicago's National League franchise went through three "official" names and more than a handful of not-so-official ones during its and the league's initial 30 years of existence. The record books had listed them first as the White Stockings, then the Black Stockings, and then the Colts. Creative sports-writers had come up with everything from "Rainmakers" (after a series of rained-out games) to "Remnants" (after several top players jumped to Chicago's new American League team, the White Sox, in 1901).

Even "Cubs" was not official for the initial five years it was used. First coined in an anonymous sports column in the March 27, 1902, *Chicago Daily News*, it alluded, as "Colts" had before it, to the youthful makeup of the current team. Fans liked the name right away, but it wasn't until players were seen wearing coats with large white bears on the sleeves during the 1907 World Series that it stuck for good.

More often than not in 1908, and most other years in the early 20th century, the Cubs walked off the field at West Side Grounds (and every other park) as winners.

Cubs Take a "Chance"— and Are Rewarded

Frank Chance debuted with the Colts in 1898, the first season in 23 years that dethroned player-manager Cap Anson was not with the club. In time, Chance, like Anson, would become a fan favorite who earned the respect of teammates through great play and an aggressive style. Nicknamed "the Peerless Leader," he would also match his predecessor's success as a player-manager by guiding the club during its most prosperous stretch since Anson's heyday in the 1880s.

Unlike many major-leaguers of the rough-and-tumble dead-ball era who came from humble beginnings, Chance was the son of a well-to-do banker in Fresno, California. He reportedly took college medical courses as a semipro catcher, and he was recommended to Anson by Colts outfielder Bill Lange as "the most promising player I ever saw." Surprisingly fast for a big man but not a strong defensive receiver, Chance was also injury prone and relegated to a backup role during his first four seasons in the majors.

Frank Selee took over as Colts manager in 1902, and he moved Chance to first base midseason. The next year was Chance's first as a starter, and he took immediate advantage. He hit .327 with 67 stolen bases and improved defense. The next season Selee named him captain, and when the manager's health failed in mid-1905, that duty was awarded to Chance as well.

The Cubs were already showing signs of championship-caliber play when Chance took over, but with the Peerless Leader at the helm, they took off. They won four pennants and two world championships from 1906 to 1910. Chance's playing time in the regular season declined late in this period, but the .296 lifetime hitter (with 401 steals) always put himself in when it counted. He compiled a .300 average in 20 World Series games. His authoritarian style turned teammates off over time— as Anson's had on his clubs—but they performed for him. Chance's .664 winning percentage as manager (on a 768–389 record) is the best in team history. In the end, despite severe hearing problems brought on by repeated beanings, his 15 seasons in Chicago concluded in 1912 with a release rather than retirement. Like Cap, he had a tough time letting go.

Chance was as tough as they came when the mood—or moment—struck him. He was not afraid to exchange fisticuffs with opponents, but his most celebrated foe may have been teammate Heinie Zimmerman, whom he once beat up despite the young player's ten-year age advantage.

A Season for the Ages: 116–36

Determined to finally overtake the Giants in Frank Chance's first full year as manager, the Cubs made some big moves heading into 1906. Trades brought in third baseman Harry Steinfeldt and outfielder Jimmy Sheckard, both of whom wound up as major contributors in the field and at the plate. The Cubs, in fact, were much improved overall on offense. After batting .245 as a team in 1905, they topped the National League with a .262 mark in '06—led by top-ten season finishers Steinfeldt (.327), Chance (.319), and catcher Johnny Kling (.312).

The pitching staff, always a strong suit, surprised even the most optimistic rooters at West Side Grounds with a team ERA of 1.75, which was nearly a full run below the league average. Three Finger Brown checked in at 1.04, leaving historians to ponder not how he won 26 games but how he managed to lose six. He was far from alone; minor-league signee Jack Pfiester, second-year man Ed Reulbach, and graybeard Carl Lundgren rounded out a stellar "Big Four" rotation, while midseason acquisitions Jack Taylor and Orval Overall also shined on the mound. Throw in Chicago's usual terrific defense, and you had a club that Albert Spalding's baseball

guide deemed "a perfected Base Ball machine that showed no weakness at any point."

They weren't quite perfect, but they were close. Just 6–6 after two weeks, the Cubs won ten straight to move into first place and were never out of the top spot after May 15. They had the pennant essentially wrapped up by August, yet they still went an almost unfathomable 50–7 (with one tie) after August 1, including winning streaks of 11, 12, and 14 games. The Giants, NL champs the previous two seasons, finished in second this time—a full 20 games behind Chance's record-setting juggernaut.

Much to the delight of Chicagoans, the opposition facing the Cubs in their

first modern World Series would be their crosstown rival White Sox. Themselves winners of 19 straight games (with one tie) in midsummer, the Sox had edged the New York Highlanders for the American League crown and finished with "just" a 93–58 record. Nobody but their own fans gave them much chance in baseball's first postseason "City Series," but then that's why they play the games.

Just how dominant were the 1906 Cubs? In addition to the major categories of batting average, ERA, and fielding, they also led the National League in total runs, hits, triples, shutouts, and strikeouts. They did finish second in stolen bases and doubles, but nobody noticed.

AS BASEBALL CARDS
GREW IN POPULARITY
EARLY IN THE 20TH
CENTURY, MORDECAI
BROWN WAS A
COVETED PLAYER
FOR COLLECTORS
YOUNG AND OLD
TO ACQUIRE.

JIMMY SHECKARD
EXCELLED AT GETTING ON
BASE FOR THE CUBS—
AND GETTING HOME. IN
1911, HE LED THE NL IN
WALKS (147) AND RUNS
SCORED (121).

SOLLY HOFMAN WAS WITH THE CUBS FROM 1904 TO
1912, DURING WHICH HE PLAYED OUTFIELD AND EVERY
INFIELD POSITION BUT CATCHER. HE HIT .325 IN 1910.

HERE IS
THE FAMOUS POEM
ABOUT TINKER, EVERS, AND CHANCE
(SEE PAGE 36) ILLUSTRATED
WITH IMAGES OF THE THREE
BALLPLAYERS.

SINCE FIRST COURTED BY "LADIES DAYS" IN THE LATE 1870S, WOMEN HAVE PROVEN ENTHUSIASTIC AND LOYAL FANS. HERE A CUBS ROOTER SHOWS HER ALLEGIANCE IN 1907.

White Sox club Cubs, capture all-Chicago Series

CHICAGO, Oct. 14, 1906—The White Sox capped a "dream" World Series for Chicago baseball fans today by defeating the Cubs, 8–3, before an estimated crowd of 25,000 at South Side Park.

The victory gave the surprising Sox a six-game triumph over their crosstown rivals, who had been heavy favorites entering the fall classic.

The normally light-hitting victors, who batted just .198 overall for the series, got plenty of offense today and sent Cubs ace Mordecai Brown to the showers in the second inning. Doc White earned the complete-game win, giving the Sox' vaunted pitching staff a 1.50 ERA for the six games.

THIS PHOTO SPREAD CELEBRATES THE 1906-07 CUBS AS "WORLD'S CHAMPIONS AND RECORD BREAKERS," A NICE WAY OF SAYING THEY WON THE 1907 WORLD SERIES BUT FELL SHORT IN 1906 DESPITE A RECORD-SETTING 116 VICTORIES DURING THE REGULAR SEASON.

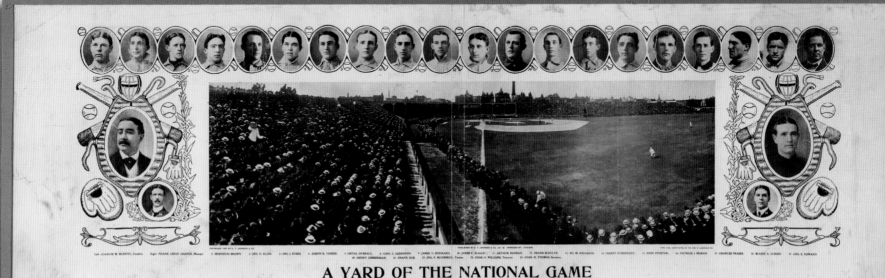

A YARD OF THE NATIONAL GAME

Chicago Baseball Club. World's Champions and Record Breakers
Winners National League Pennant 1906 and 1907, World's Pennant 1907

Brown Proves "Clincher" of Cubs

If the Cubs had one winner-take-all game to play and their first World Series appearance since 1945 hung in the balance, which pitcher from their long history should start? Current fans might pick Fergie Jenkins or Greg Maddux for the assignment, while old-timers could choose Bill Lee or Charlie Root. All were excellent hurlers, but you have to go back even further to find the best choice. Not only does Mordecai "Three Finger" Brown have the lowest ERA in team history (1.80), he has one major advantage over the others: He also won the biggest games in team history.

On October 12, 1907, Brown fashioned a seven-hit shutout against the Tigers in snowy Detroit as the Cubs captured their first World Series championship. Almost exactly a year later, after pitching in 11 of 14 contests to help the Cubs tie the New York Giants atop the National League going into the last day of the '08 regular season, he tossed eight-plus stellar innings of relief in the finale to beat Giants ace Christy

Mordecai Brown was a study in focus during the 1907 World Series at West Side Grounds, one of four fall classics in which he appeared for the Chicago Cubs. Although his post-season record was just 5–4, he compiled a fine 2.97 ERA over 57⅔ innings and won the series-clinching game in 1907.

MORDECAI PETER BROWN
(THREE-FINGERED AND MINER)
MEMBER OF CHICAGO N.L.CHAMPIONSHIP
TEAM OF 1906,'07,'08,'10.A RIGHT HANDED
PITCHER,WON 239 GAMES DURING MAJOR
LEAGUE CAREER THAT ALSO INCLUDED
ST. LOUIS AND CINCINNATI N.L.AND CLUBS
IN F.L.FIRST MAJOR LEAGUER TO PITCH
FOUR CONSECUTIVE SHUTOUTS,ACHIEVING
THIS FEAT ON JUNE 13, JUNE 25, JULY 2
AND JULY 4 IN 1908.

Ravaged by diabetes as well as a stroke, Brown missed becoming a Hall of Famer while alive. He died at age 71 in February 1948, 15 months before his selection by the Veterans Committee. He was admitted to Cooperstown along with another pretty fair hurler who led his club to a championship: Kid Nichols.

Mathewson, 4–2, and clinch the pennant before a raucous Polo Grounds crowd of between 35,000 and 40,000 (plus another 60,000 watching from Coogan's Bluff above the ballpark). The Tigers were again the opponents in the World Series that followed, and Brown won twice as Chicago captured its last world title.

Amazingly, Brown could attribute his success, which included six straight 20-win seasons for the Cubs from 1906 to 1911, to a pair of childhood mishaps that earned him his nickname. When the Nyesville, Indiana, native was seven years old, he lost his right index finger above the second knuckle and impaired his thumb and pinky permanently in his uncle's corn shredder. Just a few weeks later, he fell chasing a hog and broke the third and fourth fingers of the same hand, which healed unnaturally.

Initially a third baseman as an amateur player, Brown found that as a pitcher he could put extra spin on the ball with his shortened index and crooked middle fingers, producing a dipping, down-and-out curve that Ty Cobb called "the most devastating pitch I ever faced." It resulted in scores of harmless grounders and eventually 239 big-league wins. "That old paw served me pretty well in its time," the former coal miner said of his mangled hand, which also sent him into the Hall of Fame in 1949.

Brown was not the least bit shy about showing off his mangled right hand. He was so proud of what he accomplished with it as a pitcher that he had the corn shredder that did the damage put on display in the Terre Haute, Indiana, gas station he operated after his playing days were over.

ARMED AND DANGEROUS

While the Cubs lineup during the team's terrific 1905–1910 stretch didn't always produce runs at an extraordinary clip, it didn't often have to—the pitching staff made sure of it. During an era known for low-scoring games, Chicago still stood out with perhaps the most talented collection of arms in baseball history. Mordecai "Three Finger" Brown was the mainstay, a right-handed horse who thrived on big games and could start or relieve with equal success. Brown won 20 games five times during this period, while other hurlers including Ed Reulbach, Orval Overall, Jack Pfiester, and Carl Lundgren also topped or neared the magic figure on several occasions. As a team, the Cubs had the lowest ERA in the National League each of the six seasons except 1908, and they shut out opponents an incredible 162 times during the span—leading the circuit each year.

Orval Overall

"Tinker to Evers to Chance"

Baseball is the most literary of games, perhaps because it has no clock and moves at a slower pace, thus allowing fans—and writers—to more closely watch drama unfold and personalities emerge. First baseman Frank Chance, shortstop Joe Tinker, and second baseman John Evers played alongside one another in the Cubs infield for parts of 11 years, and the elegant efficiency with which they worked together through the long spans of the seasons was captured by newspaper columnist Franklin Pierce Adams in a poem he entitled "Baseball's Sad Lexicon." It appeared in the *New York Evening Mail* on July 10, 1910, apparently only because his editor said another article Adams had written for that edition was too short and they needed one more piece to fill the space. This is what the Chicago native submitted:

> *These are the saddest of possible words:*
> *"Tinker to Evers to Chance."*
> *Trio of bear cubs, and fleeter than birds,*
> *Tinker and Evers and Chance.*
> *Ruthlessly pricking our gonfalon bubble,*
> *Making a Giant hit into a double-*
> *Words that are heavy with nothing*
> > *but trouble:*
> *"Tinker to Evers to Chance."*

Nearly a century later, it remains likely the most famous prose ever written about any sport—rivaled only by "Casey at the Bat" (which was about a fictional character). Because action photos of early 20th century baseball are scarce and film even rarer, we have little but the imagery created by writers to help us envision the athleticism of players from the dead-ball era. But reading this poem, one

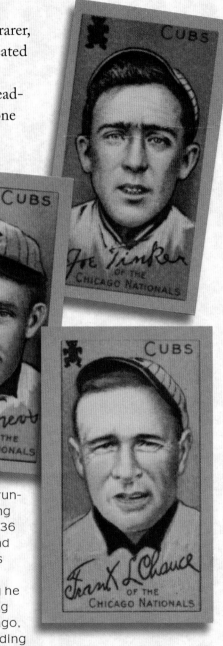

Top: His .262 lifetime batting average is among the lowest of any Hall of Famer, but Joe Tinker could hit the very best—compiling a much higher mark against great Giants hurler Christy Mathewson. A strong defensive player and baserunner, he led NL shortstops in fielding percentage four times and stole 336 bases. *Middle:* Whether tiny second baseman John Evers deserved his 1946 Hall of Fame recognition is debatable, but there is no denying he was a winner. In addition to playing with three NL champions in Chicago, he was the league's MVP after leading the "Miracle Braves" to the 1914 NL title and hitting .438 in a stunning World Series sweep of the Athletics. *Bottom:* Considered by many the only "true" Hall of Famer among the famous trio elected to Coopers-town together in 1946, Frank Chance was arguably "Hall-worthy" as both a player and manager. He didn't live to enjoy either distinction, however, dying of tuberculosis at age 48 in 1924.

Originally a catcher, the husky Chance *(at left, below)* could still go into a crouch when necessary as a first baseman. Despite being quite big for his era (6'0", 190 pounds), he was a quick runner who led the National League in stolen bases with 67 in 1903 and 57 in 1906.

can almost picture the Chicago double play, starting with a grounder to short.

They were not always the best of friends—Tinker and Evers, in fact, once supposedly went several years without speaking off the field—but on the diamond they were in total sync. And while there were certainly far more than three standout performers on the terrific Cubs of 1906–13, thanks to Franklin Pierce Adams, this trio of bear cubs always got top billing—right up until their Hall of Fame election (together, of course) in 1946. Especially in light of Tinker's career batting average (.262), some credit Adams for their selection as well.

HARRY STEINFELDT: MAN WITHOUT A POEM

If ever a man had a right to hate a piece of poetry, Cubs third baseman Harry Steinfeldt was the man—and the famous tribute to his Chicago infield mates by Franklin Pierce Adams was the ballad. In addition to likely helping its three protagonists into the Hall of Fame, the poem also doomed to anonymity the excellent ballplayer who toiled alongside them.

Steinfeldt hit .327 with a league-high 83 RBI and 176 hits for the pennant-winning Cubs of 1906. As a starter on four World Series teams, he batted .471 in Chicago's win over Detroit in the 1907 Fall Classic. He was also an excellent fielder and basestealer. Despite all these contributions to the Cubs—not to mention eight more solid seasons with the Cincinnati Reds—he is today remembered primarily by trivia buffs who stump their bar mates by asking, "Who played alongside Tinker, Evers, and Chance?" Harry deserves better.

Here, in its glorious order from left to right, is the top-notch infield that led the Cubs to four pennants in five years: Steinfeldt (3B), Tinker (SS), Evers (2B), and Chance (1B). One of them, however, was left out of Franklin Pierce Adam's poem and the Hall of Fame. Notice who's not smiling?

World Series Glory 1907:
Cubs Pitching Declaws Tigers

After their six-game loss to the White Sox in the 1906 World Series—an outcome that shocked the baseball world, not to mention the team itself—the Cubs were determined to prove their mettle as the game's greatest franchise by making a return trip with different results.

First they had to get through the regular season of 1907, which in many ways was a carbon copy of the previous year. Although Chicago didn't hit quite as well, the pitching was almost identically stellar. The team ERA went down just a shade, from 1.75 to 1.73, and once again dwarfed the league average and nearest runner-up (Pittsburgh). The Pirates were also second to the Cubs in the NL standings, but as with the Giants the year before, it wasn't close. Chicago went 13–2 in April, was near its record 116-win pace into July, and by mid-August had an insurmountable 14-game lead. The final margin was 17 games; the final record 107–45.

Even more so than in 1906, when several players had sparkling statistics, this was a team effort. There was no .300 hitter in the Chicago lineup and nobody with more than 70 RBI. Their World Series opponents, the Detroit Tigers, had a pair of Hall of Fame outfielders with far gaudier stats: veteran Sam Crawford (.323 average) and 20-year-old Ty Cobb (an American League-best .350 with 119 RBI). But with a 92–58 record and just a 1¹/₂-game margin of victory in the AL, the Tigers were considered underdogs. The Cubs, of course, were in no mood to surprise the oddsmakers again.

In the end, they didn't. The first Series game ended in a 3–3 tie when darkness halted play in the 12th inning at West Side Grounds, but Chicago took Games 2 and 3 at home behind complete games from Jack Pfiester (3–1) and Ed Ruelbach (5–1). Orval Overall also went the distance for the Cubs in a 6–1 win in Game 4 at Detroit, and Three Finger Brown completed the sweep with a seven-hit, 2–0 shutout in the finale. Cobb (with a .200 Series average) and Crawford (.238) had been kept quiet, and the West Side Boys had been

Below: It lacked the excitement of the all-Chicago classic the previous fall, but the 1907 World Series was far more satisfying for Cubs fans. After losing three home games in the '06 series, the superstitious Cubs wore their road gray uniforms for Game 1 this time, but the game wound up a 3–3 tie. *Bottom:* The Cubs were back in their home whites for Games 2 and 3 of the '07 World Series, and this time the luck was good, with 3–1 and 5–1 victories delivered by pitchers Jack Pfiester and Ed Reulbach, respectively.

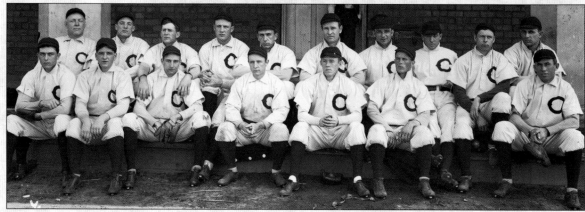

World Series Glory 1908: Cubs Top Tigers Again for Last Series Win

The Cubs were a year more seasoned in 1908, but that didn't result in the returning world champions having another easy time of things in the National League. Although Tinker, Evers, Chance, and company were all back, it would take one of the wildest and most controversial plays in league history to help Chicago claim its third straight pennant.

The Cubs had bolted out to huge leads in the previous two seasons, but the '08 campaign proved a tougher and more entertaining race. The Pirates and Giants, distant runners-up to Chicago in its last two NL romps, managed to keep things much tighter. The three clubs were neck and neck all summer. Going into September, the Cubs and Giants were tied for the top spot with Pittsburgh a half-game back. Things stayed close throughout that month and into October, each team playing well over .700 ball for the period.

Things came down to the final day for all three teams. The Pirates bowed out with a 5–2 loss at Chicago on October 4, leaving them a half-game behind. The Cubs and Giants, who finished the regular season tied, met at the Polo Grounds on October 8 for a single playoff game to determine the pennant winner. New York went up 1–0 against Cubs starter Jack Pfiester in the first, but Three Finger Brown came in to snuff out the rally.

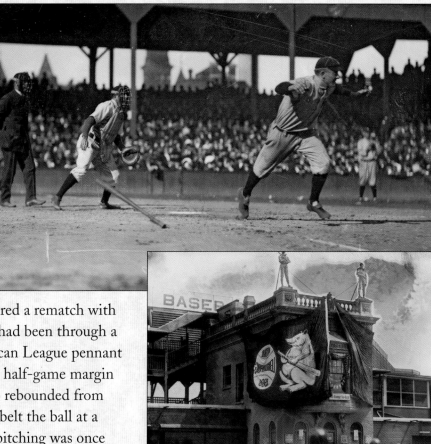

Brown went the rest of the way, and big hits by Tinker (a triple), Frank "Wildfire" Schulte, and Chance (back-to-back doubles) off Giants 37-game winner Christy Mathewson gave Chicago a 4–2 win and the pennant.

The World Series offered a rematch with the Detroit Tigers, who had been through a similarly stressful American League pennant race before escaping by a half-game margin over Cleveland. Ty Cobb rebounded from his dreadful '06 series to belt the ball at a .368 clip, but Chicago's pitching was once again too much for the Tigers. Orval Overall allowed just seven hits and one run in a pair of complete-game wins, while the tireless Brown pitched a four-hit shutout in Game 4 and won the opener in relief. His 0.00 ERA and Chance's .421 average were huge factors in Chicago's five-game win, the second—and second straight—world championship for the Cubs. Little did fans know how long their children and grandchildren would be waiting for the team's *next* world championship.

Top: Ty Cobb, batting here at West Side Grounds, hit much better in the 1908 World Series than he had the previous year, and he even added a few stolen bases. It wasn't enough, however, to stop the Cubs from becoming the first team in the modern era to win two consecutive world championships. *Above:* The wooden West Side Grounds may have been showing signs of age by 1908, but it still looked grand when "dressed up" during World Series time.

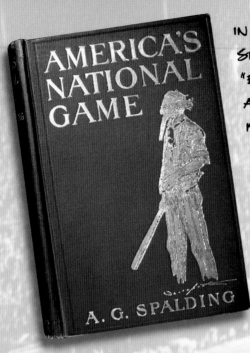

IN HIS 1911 BOOK, SPALDING DECLARED "BASE BALL IS THE AMERICAN GAME PAR EXCELLENCE, BECAUSE ITS PLAYING DEMANDS BRAIN AND BRAWN, AND AMERICAN MANHOOD SUPPLIES THESE INGREDIENTS."

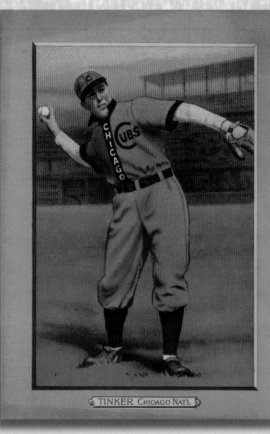

JUDGING FROM JOE TINKER'S UNIFORM, THIS PAINTING PROBABLY DATES FROM 1909, WHEN "CHICAGO" WAS ADDED DOWN THE JERSEY FRONT AND THE FAMILIAR BEAR LOGO WAS REPLACED WITH "CUBS."

IN 1910, EACH ATHLETICS PLAYER RECEIVED A $2,068 WINNER'S SHARE FOR BEATING CHICAGO IN THE WORLD SERIES. BY 2007, PROGRAMS FROM THE SERIES WERE SELLING FOR $5,000-$10,000.

ON AUGUST 22, 1912, THE CUBS SCORED 17 RUNS TO BEAT THE BOSTON BRAVES—AND THAT KEPT A FAN BUSY MARKING UP AN OFFICIAL SCORE CARD LIKE THIS ONE.

REACH GOODS MAKE FAMOUS PLAYERS

EVERS   ZIMMERMAN   TINKER

Reach
Fielders'
Mitts

13

SUCCESS MEANT THE OPPORTUNITY TO
PICK UP EXTRA CASH FROM PRODUCT
ENDORSEMENTS, AS THREE CUBS
STARS DID IN THIS 1913 ADVERTISEMENT.

NATIONAL LEAGUE
OFFICIAL SCORE CARD
CHICAGO
1903
5¢

SOLD EXCLUSIVELY ON THE GROUNDS

PUBLIC
AND
PLAYERS
CHOICE

BLUE
RIBBON
PEPSIN
GUM

FLAVORS
PEPSIN.
MINT.
LICORICE.
BLOOD ORANGE

This is Our Trade Mark
·Cracker·Jack·
THE NEW CONFECTION
R

Mfd by D.W. NORRIS, Chicago.

Atlas
BREWING CO.
OUR BRANDS
"GENUINE
BOHEMIAN BEER"

TEL. CANAL 967.
KING OF TONICS
Peptomaltene

"MAGNET
AND
EXPORT"
HAVE NO EQUAL.

SOLD BY ALL
LEADING DRUGGISTS.

TEL. MAIN 1436.
Murray & Co.
CHICAGO, ILL.
MADISON ST. COR. MARKET
TENTS.
AWNINGS,
FLAGS,   SIGNS OF EVERY DESCRIPTION.   CAMP FURNITURE.
CANVAS GOODS,

THIS SCORE
CARD IS FROM
1903, WHEN THE
CUBS WON 82
GAMES AND LOST
56. DESPITE A
.594 WINNING
PERCENTAGE,
THEY FINISHED IN
THIRD PLACE.

A REPLICA 1911 JERSEY SHOWCASES THE
EARLY CUB LOGO OF A BEAR HOLDING
A BAT.

Cubs shut down Cobb to top Tigers

DETROIT, Oct. 12, 1907—Holding Ty Cobb to just one hit and his teammates to only six more, the Cubs finished off a one-sided World Series today with a 2–0 victory before a small crowd of 7,370 at Bennett Park.

The shutout by Chicago's Modecai Brown was the big story this afternoon, but the key to the Cubs' five-game triumph was stopping the dangerous Cobb. The AL batting champ and stolen-base king was held to a .200 average during the Series, drove in no runs, and was thrown out by catcher Johnny Kling in his only two steal attempts.

Chance's Last Stand: The 1910 Pennant

Catcher Johnny Kling left the Cubs after the team's three successive pennants of 1906–08, choosing to sit out the 1909 season and focus on his pocket billiards career. Chicago still managed to win 104 games without him, but this impressive total was only good for second place—six games behind slugging shortstop Honus Wagner and his peaking Pittsburgh Pirates.

Kling was back for 1910, however, and with the usual steady veteran performances and prolific production from outfielders Wildfire Schulte (a league-leading ten homers) and Solly Hofman (a .325 average, third in the NL) the Cubs managed to duplicate their 104 victories of the previous year and capture yet another pennant. Led by Three Finger Brown, the pitching staff was once again outstanding. Chicago's eventual 13-game

advantage over second-place New York was likely extra satisfying to Cubs players who remembered finishing behind the Giants by this same margin in both 1904 and '05.

The only major setback during the regular season was a broken leg suffered by Johnny Evers late in the summer, which put him on the shelf for the World Series. Even without its star second baseman, Chicago was once again a fall classic favorite. Manager Connie Mack's Philadelphia Athletics had won the American League title behind infield stars Eddie Collins and Frank Baker and a pitching staff that rivaled the Cubs in excellence, but the A's were still a young club lacking postseason experience.

For the second time in five years, however, the Cubs failed to live up to expectations. Philadelphia captured the first two games

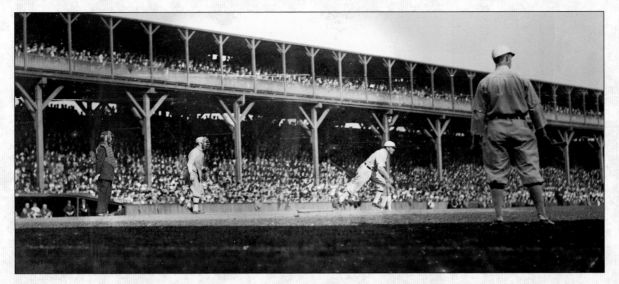

On June 2, 1908, Cub teammates Jimmy Sheckard *(pictured above running to first)* and Heinie Zimmerman got into a fistfight that escalated into a throwing match. Heinie heaved a glass bottle of ammonia that burst when it hit Jimmy right between the eyes, and Sheckard was nearly blinded. He was out several weeks but recovered to play in that fall's World Series.

at home, 4–1 and 9–3, breaking the second contest open with a six-run seventh inning. Another big inning—a five-run third—doomed Chicago in Game 3 as the A's

embarrassed them at West Side Grounds 12–5. Philadelphia was one inning away from a sweep before the Cubs rallied for a 4–3, ten-inning win in the fourth contest, but 31-game winner Jack Coombs hurled his third complete-game victory of the Series the next day to finish off Chicago. The Cubs would still have some contending seasons left in them, but the Series had revealed them for what they were—an aging club about to go into decline.

JOHNNY KLING, HALL OF FAMER?

Because catchers are central to the outcome of every game, logic dictates that Johnny Kling was a major figure during the greatest stretch in Cubs history. Behind the plate for Chicago's 1906–08 and 1910 pennant winners, he was a strong hitter and the top defensive receiver of his era. Modest and soft-spoken, he batted .312 for the record-breaking 1906 club, twice stole 23 bases, and was deemed by Cubs pitcher Ed Reulbach as "one of the greatest catchers who ever wore a mask." Other teammates similarly praised his ability and baseball smarts.

Each year, starting with the first Hall of Fame election in 1936, Kling appeared on a small but respectable number of sportswriters' ballots. Though he was denied admission, those votes recognized his notable achievements. By the early 1950s, however, his name had dropped off the list entirely. Now, with a special Cooperstown committee reexamining his career and that of other old-timers, Kling will get another shot at joining teammates Tinker, Evers, Chance, and Brown in immortality.

Charles Murphy: Perfect Timing, Imperfect Owner

Anybody who buys into a sports franchise hopes to do so just as it is on the cusp of greatness. By purchasing the Cubs in July 1905, Charles Murphy hit the jackpot. Starting the next year, the team won four pennants and two World Series titles over five seasons, and they stayed a consistent winner until he sold out in 1914. Still, despite the franchise's success, Murphy enraged his ballplayers, fellow owners, and Chicago fans with his pompous demeanor.

A pharmacist-turned-sportswriter who liked to hang around big-wheelers, Murphy eventually got paid to do so with the 1905 New York Giants as the first press agent employed by a major-league club. While traveling on the road with the team,

Charles Murphy grew increasingly unpopular with Cubs players, fans, and fellow National League owners during his troubled tenure. By 1913, he was in no mood to cooperate with a photographer disturbing his private box at West Side Grounds.

he overheard that the Cubs were going up for sale. He immediately took a midnight train to meet Chicago owner James Hart. Murphy negotiated a deal that enabled him to purchase the team for $105,000 on a loan from Charles Taft, whom he had befriended while working at the Cincinnati *Times-Star* (which Taft owned).

Installed as president, replacing Hart, Murphy was soon feuding with other owners who saw him as a lout who was in the papers too much and couldn't be trusted. He was also viewed as cheap. He wouldn't build a visiting team clubhouse at West Side Grounds, was reprimanded for scalping World Series tickets for a profit in 1908, and even antagonized sportswriters (not a good idea) by seating them in the last row of the grandstands during that series. "Charles Murphy…has no sentiment for baseball, only for the money there may be in it for him," wrote Sam Crane of the New York *Evening Journal*. "In fact, the 'Chubby One' is considered a joke all over the National League, and nowhere more so than in Chicago."

By 1914, after Murphy had further enraged fans by calling his players drunks and engaging in very public disputes with infield greats Frank Chance and Johnny Evers, the other NL owners had endured enough. A deal was worked out in which Murphy could sell his stock to Taft for $500,000.

A Day at the Ballpark, 1908

Those who had the pleasure of attending Cubs games during the first decade of the 20th century saw the team at its apex, but the venue they played in was nothing special. West Side Grounds in 1908 was one of many wooden ballparks then populating the major-league landscape, with the beginning of the steel-and-concrete era (which would include Wrigley Field) still a year or two away. Many seats still cost 25 cents, but since factory workers were often making $1 a day or less, this was far from throwaway change.

Coats and ties remained the preferred ballpark dress, with long dresses for the ladies. Women had been a novelty sighting at games a decade or two back, but they were now more commonplace and easily recognizable by the enormous hats that were then in style (and could, on occasion, result in complaints from fans blocked from viewing the action on the field). "Take Me Out to the Ballgame," a popular song about fictional fan Katie Casey, was written and debuted this year.

There was still no alcohol sold at games in Chicago, but there was plenty of soda, lemonade, peanuts, candy, and even cigars to purchase from roaming vendors. Horse-and-carriage arrivals at the ballpark were down, bus and subway arrivals were up. Although the Model T came out this year and would soon multiply, most fans still did not own automobiles.

Even when not at the ballpark, fans now had a number of ways to follow baseball.

Daily newspapers were expanding their coverage, and evening editions often carried partial or full boxscores from the same day's games. In addition, spectators could gather in downtown squares and other venues to "watch" ballgames on huge electronic scoreboards updated by workers getting the action by telegraph. On the day of the 1908 pennant playoff between the Cubs and Giants, one of these boards was set up in Chicago's Thomas Orchestra Hall, where a crowd, which included player-manager Frank Chance's wife, celebrated the Cubs victory.

Top: Sometimes the normal confines of cozy West Side Grounds were not enough to accommodate the huge throngs of fans clamoring to see the Cubs in action. Here, at a 1908 game, is a view of the solution, letting fans stand on the field just beyond the outfield playing area. *Above:* Fans line up outside the Cubs team offices at West Side Grounds to purchase tickets in this 1908 photo. The '08 world championship team drew 665,325 fans, one of 11 straight years it finished first or second in attendance among the National League's eight clubs.

CHAPTER THREE

THE DRY YEARS: 1914–1925

FRESH OFF THE greatest stretch in their history, the Cubs moved from the West Side to the North, but they failed to continue their winning ways in a new neighborhood and ballpark. They did earn a lone pennant in 1918, but it was tainted by America's involvement in World War I.

Left: A slick-fielding, heavy-hitting shortstop, Charlie Hollocher was often out of the lineup and in the headlines due to a chronic stomach ailment that baffled doctors. He hit .316 as a 1918 rookie and .340 in '22, but he was forced to retire at age 28. When he committed suicide in 1940, his wife said the old pain had returned. *Right:* Before taking the field for their first Opening Day at Weeghman Park on April 20, 1916, the Cubs delighted the crowd by marching across the diamond with members of the four brass bands invited to the festivities.

Cubs Experience Growing Pains in Move to North Side

Cubs fans, who had been spoiled during the first dozen years of the 20th century, would have a bit rougher go of it during the next 12 years. After watching their team compete for the National League pennant almost every season and win the flag on four occasions, they would see it struggle through a period of immense change on and off the field.

Heroes Joe Tinker, Johnny Evers, Frank Chance, Johnny Kling, and Mordecai Brown, each of whom had graced West Side Grounds for the bulk of a decade, were all gone by 1914. Their replacements had amusing names, such as Hippo Vaughn, Heinie Zimmerman, and Zip Zabel. While some of these players became stars in their own right, the string of championships and near misses came to an end. In 1915, the team compiled its first

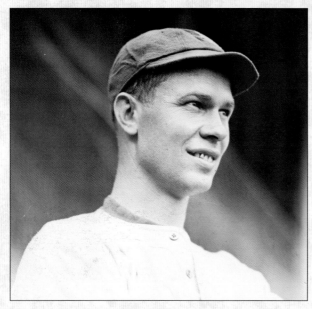

Just 12–14 as a Cub, George "Zip" Zabel had one remarkable outing: On June 17, 1915, the right-hander set a record for most relief innings pitched in one game. Coming in for starter Bert Humphries with two outs in the first, he pitched the final 18⅓ innings as Chicago outlasted the Dodgers, 4–3. Jeff Pfeffer went the distance for Brooklyn.

Third baseman Heinie Zimmerman led the NL with a .372 average and 14 homers in 1912, but his figure of 103 RBI has been disputed. Not a "true" statistic at the time, runs batted in were not always neatly tabulated. Some claim Heinie had just 99—third to Honus Wagner's 102. So Zimmerman *may* have won the Triple Crown.

losing record in 13 years. It would finish below the break-even point five more times in the next decade. West Side Grounds, scene of many great triumphs, was growing old and outdated.

The club's leadership was also in flux. Chance had been manager for seven-plus seasons during the team's heyday, but the Cubs were now in the midst of five different skippers in a five-year span. And while most folks didn't mind seeing despised owner Charles Murphy ousted from his post by his major-league brethren, the two other Charleses who succeeded him—first Charles Thomas, then Charles Weeghman—would have their own challenges keeping fans happy and making a profit. If this wasn't problematic enough, in 1914 a new team came to town (the Federal League's Chicago Whales), raiding the Cubs for players and fans.

But while there wouldn't be any enduring poetry written about this Cubs team, things did eventually start to improve. The Federal League folded after two years, which led to the Cubs getting a new owner (Weeghman) and a new ballpark on the city's growing North Side. World War I hurt all major-league clubs—losing men to the military—but the group left on Chicago's National League roster was able to capture a pennant in the war-shortened 1918 season. New heroes emerged, including Vaughn and Grover Cleveland Alexander in the pitching ranks, and Charlie Hollocher, Ray Grimes, and Jigger Statz in the everyday lineup. And when Weeghman's failing restaurant business forced him to sell the club, it was to a minority owner who would bring the franchise first stability, then success: William Wrigley, Jr.

It all added up to a period of transition that didn't produce much in the way of winning baseball but was necessary for the Cubs to move forward. Wrigley and his hand-plucked president, William Veeck, Sr., were determined to give Chicago fans a team that could remain competitive over the long haul, but it would take some time to get there.

THE WRIGLEY EMPIRE

Chewing gum was very kind to William Wrigley, Jr. In addition to the Wrigley Company itself—with its factories in five countries—the businessman's holdings in the 1920s and early '30s included the Cubs, the minor-league Los Angeles Angels of the Pacific Coast League, the Arizona Biltmore Hotel, and mansions near Phoenix and in Pasadena, California. Then there is the world-famous Wrigley Building in downtown Chicago, symbolizing, as the first office structure built north of the Chicago River outside the "loop," his vision for business growth. Not bad for a guy who came to the city with $32 in his pocket.

Wrigley Building (left), downtown Chicago

Wrigley devised a great way to get one Chicago sportswriter to praise his team: He made him an executive. *Chicago American* reporter Bill Veeck, Sr. *(pictured above)*, was named Cubs vice president in 1918, and then president the next year. The former scribe ran the club in a general manager-like capacity through 1933, returning it to contender status.

Unpopular Cubs minority owner/president Charles Murphy was forced to step down and sell his shares in 1914 by other NL bosses upset with his treatment of players and managers. Charles Thomas *(shown here)* served as a "stop-gap" president until majority owner, Charles Taft, could sell the franchise. When he did, Thomas was history.

The Federal League
Flourishes in Chicago

It didn't last long, but while it did Chicagoans got the most out of the Federal League (FL), including two thrilling pennant races and a storied ballpark.

Formed in 1913 by a group of wealthy businessmen hoping to financially benefit from America's growing fascination with baseball, the FL operated for one year as a minor-league operation, then billed itself as the third major league starting in 1914. It enticed American and National League stars to "jump" to its ranks with higher salaries and the promise that they could be "free agents"

in future seasons. Many athletes who felt imprisoned by the reserve clause, which gave AL and NL owners full control over where they played, took the offer.

The 1914 Federal League season began with teams in Chicago and seven other cities: Baltimore, Brooklyn, Buffalo, Kansas City, Pittsburgh, St. Louis, and Indianapolis. New ballparks were built for each club, and former Cubs shortstop great Joe Tinker became one of the most-heralded "jumpers" by joining the Chicago Whales as player-manager. Also known as the Chi-Feds, the Whales,

The 1914 Whales (or Chi-Feds) were led offensively by outfielder Dutch Zwilling, who paced the club with a .313 average, 16 homers, and 95 RBI but couldn't stick with the Cubs after the Federal League folded. Top pitcher Claude Hendrix (29–10), however, later went 20–7 for Chicago's 1918 NL champs.

CHIFEDS

Joe Tinker's .256 average as player-manager of the Chi-Feds in 1914 was a big drop-off from his previous year's .317 mark with the Cubs, but he was still a fan favorite. Worn down at age 34 by his aggressive playing style, he was never a regular again.

owned by Charles Weeghman, finished their first season with an 87–67 record, just 1½ games behind the pennant-winning Indianapolis Hoosiers in a race decided the final week.

Although the Federal League drew well, attendance in all three leagues was hurt by the overabundance of teams, especially in those regions with two or even three clubs. (The Cubs, for instance, saw their crowds cut in half while Chicago was a three-team town.) Competing with the noncontending Cubs and White Sox, the Whales ruled Chicago in 1915 and battled with FL foes St. Louis and Pittsburgh in a race that came down to the last day. "Whales Win Pennant as 34,000 Cheer," the *Chicago Tribune* trumpeted on October 4, and among those getting the accolades was former Cubs great Three Finger Brown, a 17-game winner for the Chi-Feds.

AL and NL owners didn't like being hurt at the gate or the pocketbook (they had been forced to raise salaries to stop players from jumping to Federal clubs), and their Fed counterparts had filed an antitrust suit against Organized Baseball for their right to exist. The end result was a peace settlement after the '15 season that marked the end of the third league, but Chicago had something special to show for the Federal experiment: They had Weeghman Park, known today as Wrigley Field.

The biggest name to join the Whales in their second and last season was 38-year-old Mordecai Brown, who went 17-8 with a 2.09 ERA to help lead the 1915 club to the Federal League pennant. He returned to the Cubs the next year after the FL/NL "peace agreement," but he retired 48⅓ innings later at age 39.

THE CITY SERIES

Although the Cubs and White Sox have only met once in the World Series, for many years starting in 1903, the crosstown rivals engaged in "City Series" games during each October unless one (or both) made the fall classic. The bad blood between the National League and the upstart American League was still very strong, and crowds of 10,000 or more routinely attended these exhibition contests split between the two teams' ballparks.

And while the Cubs had usually enjoyed the better regular season, the White Sox often had their number in the match-ups, which lasted as long as 15 games. There was fiscal incentive for the players—the teams split the gate receipts, with the winners getting a bigger share—and both clubs played hard. In 1925, for instance, pitchers Grover Cleveland Alexander and Ted Blankenship each hurled all 19 innings of the City Series opener, which ended in a 2–2 tie due to darkness. Was it worth it? With nearly $600 awaiting each winning player, they thought so.

LARRY DOYLE
2nd B.—Chicago Cubs
44

VIC SAIER
1st B.—Chicago Cubs
148

CUBS
CHICAGO NATIONAL LEAGUE BALL CLUB
SEASON 1921
Champions National League 1906 1907 1908 1910 1918
10¢ OFFICIAL SCORE CARD
WM. L. VEECK, PRES.

COMPLETE
The SPORTING PAGE of THE DAILY NEWS

GROVER ALEXANDER, DEPICTED HERE ON A 1921 SCORECARD, WAS ONE OF THE FEW THINGS FANS OF THE SEVENTH-PLACE CUBS HAD TO CHEER ABOUT THAT YEAR.

THE NATIONAL LEAGUE'S MVP IN 1912, LARRY DOYLE HAD ONE SUBPAR YEAR IN CHICAGO (1917) SANDWICHED BETWEEN 13 MOSTLY STELLAR CAMPAIGNS WITH THE GIANTS.

FIRST BASEMAN VIC SAIER FINISHED IN THE NL'S TOP FIVE IN HOMERS FROM 1913 TO '15, AND HE ALSO HAD A LEAGUE-HIGH 21 TRIPLES IN 1913.

HE EXCHANGED HIS CUBS UNIFORM FOR FEDERAL LEAGUE DUDS IN 1914, BUT JOE TINKER WAS STILL THE ENVY OF YOUNGSTERS THROUGHOUT CHICAGO.

Cubs outlast Phillies in record-setting slugfest, 26–23

CHICAGO, Aug. 25, 1922—The home team did its best to prove the old adage that no lead is safe at Cubs Park, nearly blowing a 19-run advantage in a 26–23 victory over the Phillies.

Chicago scored 10 times in the second and 14 in the fourth to go up 25–6. The Cubs still led 26–9 through seven, but the Phils staged a furious rally before Tiny Osbourne struck out Bevo LeBourveau with the bases loaded to end the game. Records were set for most combined runs (49) and hits (51) by two teams in one contest, while the 14-run fourth set another mark.

CUBS PRESIDENT WILLIAM VEECK WAS PICTURED ON 1921 SCORE CARDS, WHEN THE CUBS ENDED THE SEASON 64-89.

CUBS
CHICAGO NATIONAL LEAGUE BALL CLUB
SEASON 1921
Champions National League 1906 1907 1908 1910 1918
Champions of the World 1907-1908
10¢ OFFICIAL SCORE CARD
WM. L. VEECK, PRES.

FINAL
THE BOX SCORE EDITION of THE DAILY NEWS

HE TIED FOR THE NL LEAD WITH 12 LONGBALLS IN 1916, BUT CY WILLIAMS REACHED FAR GREATER HOME RUN HEIGHTS AFTER LEAVING CHICAGO: 41 IN 1923.

A LUMBERING 6'4" LEFT-HANDER WHOSE LATE-CAREER GIRTH EARNED HIM HIS NICKNAME, JIM "HIPPO" VAUGHN WON 20 GAMES FIVE TIMES FOR CHICAGO FROM 1914 TO 1919.

No hits through nine is not enough for Vaughn, Cubs

CHICAGO, May 22, 1917—After nine spectacular innings of no-hit ball by both starting pitchers, the Reds beat the Cubs today after finally getting to Hippo Vaughn for two safeties and one run in the tenth frame at Weeghman Park. Fred Toney completed his no-hitter to earn the 1–0 win for the visitors.

Larry Kopf had singled to right with one out in the tenth for Cincinnati's first hit and then went to third on a fly-ball error by Cy Williams. Vaughn fielded Jim Thorpe's chopper in front of the plate, but catcher Art Wilson dropped his throw home—and Kopf was safe.

THE 1924 CUBS POSED FOR THE CAMERA AND FANS. THOUGH OVER .500, FINISHING THE SEASON AT 81–72, THEY WERE FIFTH IN THE LEAGUE.

Weeghman in, West Side Out

From the ruins of the Federal League the Cubs gained a new majority owner and a new ballpark. Luncheonette king Charles Weeghman, a local success story whose Chicago Whales/Chi-Feds won the second and last FL title in 1915, had built a steel-and-concrete park for his team on a North Side block bounded by Clark, Addison, Waveland, and Sheffield. Weeghman Park was constructed in just seven weeks for $250,000. It was designed by the same architect, Zachary Taylor Davis, who had drawn up the impressive Comiskey Park, home of the White Sox, a few years before.

Its namesake was delighted when an overflow crowd of 21,000 turned out for the Chi-Feds' first opener against Kansas City on April 23, 1914, especially when hearing that just 800 had watched the National League Cubs host the Reds at the old West Side Grounds that same afternoon. Such success didn't sit right with the old baseball establishment, however, and when Federal League owners agreed to fold after the 1915 season, part of their settlement deal with their AL/NL brethren allowed Weeghman and nine fellow investors to purchase controlling interest in the Cubs from owner Charles Taft. Soon after, Weeghman announced that the club (a sub-.500, fourth-place finisher the previous year) would be moving north to his ballpark from West Side Grounds, a decaying relic from the fast-fading days of wooden parks.

The first National League game at newly named Cubs Park on April 20, 1916, saw the hosts beat the Cincinnati Reds 7–6 before 18,000. Fans enjoyed the convenience of a facility that was easily accessible by both the Milwaukee Railroad and the elevated trains, and Cubs home attendance for the year more than doubled to 453,685. Fan expectations for the club were very high early on, as a group of players from Chicago's Federal League champs of '15 had been added to the roster, including former Cubs pitching ace Three Finger Brown and shortstop-manager Joe Tinker. Unfortunately, these aging stars performed more like flounders than Whales, and the result was a drop to fifth place.

Charles Weeghman is largely forgotten as the man who built Wrigley Field. Cubs majority owner from 1916 to '18, he helped assemble an NL championship squad but was soon forced to borrow heavily from minority owner William Wrigley due to financial straits. "Spendthrift Charlie" sold out completely to the chewing gum king in 1918.

Shortly after this major construction of Weeghman Park was completed in 1914, tweaks to the facility were already being made. Nine home runs were hit in the first three-game series between the Chi-Feds and Kansas City Packers, so the outfield walls were moved back: 35 feet in left, almost 50 feet in left-center.

A Pennant Amid the Peril

George "Dode" Paskert was a fine outfielder who hit .264 over 354 games for the Cubs, but his acquisition from the Phillies was eventually regretted in Chicago. The man swapped for Paskert was Cy Williams, who became just the third player—after Babe Ruth and Rogers Hornsby—to swat 250 career homers.

Bonding as a team during a period of national turmoil, the Cubs gave their fans a brief burst of joy in 1918.

Consecutive fifth-place finishes had owner Charles Weeghman desperate to turn things around, and three trades in a one-month period during the winter of 1917–18 brought in a quartet of key players: centerfielder George "Dode" Paskert, catcher Bill Killefer, and pitchers Lefty Tyler and Grover Alexander. The Alexander deal, which cost Chicago two ballplayers and a then-record $60,000, was seen as the biggest. Alexander had gone 30–13 in '17, his third straight 30-win year. It was hoped he would do more of the same for the Cubs, but the war in Europe, which the United States had entered the previous April, intervened. Alexander was drafted into the army, and he reported for duty on April 30 after just three starts and two victories.

A Cubs collapse was feared, but strong performances throughout the lineup and pitching corps kept this from occurring. On the mound, aided by seasoned catcher Killefer, Hippo Vaughn won 22 games and Tyler and Claude Hendrix each had 19 as Chicago overcame Alexander's absence to lead the league with a 2.18 team ERA that evoked memories of the great 1905–10 staffs. Offensively, rookie shortstop Charlie Hollocher hit .316 with 26 stolen bases, while first baseman Fred Merkle and outfielders Paskert and Les Mann also shined. The Cubs moved into first place on June 6 while playing in Philadelphia and never relinquished the spot, going 33–11 in one midseason stretch. They eventually won the league by 10½ games.

Unfortunately, things outside Weeghman Park were not going as smoothly. The war intensified, and baseball's National Commission governing body declared on August 1 that the regular season would end a month early on Labor Day. This was to comply with a federal "Work or Fight" order decreeing that all men of draft age join the military or find a war-related job. The Cubs clinched the pennant on August 24 and prepared to meet the Boston Red Sox in the World Series, but the fall classic would be overshadowed—justly so—by the bloodshed in Europe.

A 24-game winner with the Pirates who jumped to Chicago's Federal League squad, right-hander Claude Hendrix was picked up by the Cubs and had four losing seasons in the next five years. His one winning campaign, however, was a big one: 20–7 with 21 complete games and a 2.78 ERA for the 1918 NL champs.

Weeghman out, Wrigley In

In building up a business empire from the $32 he brought to Chicago in 1893, Wrigley placed a large emphasis on advertising. Blanketing magazines, newspapers, and storefronts with his chewing gum logo—and the cartoonish characters that appeared with it—he established unparalleled brand-name recognition.

Fresh off a World Series setback and the end of World War I, Cubs fans got another big piece of information to chew on in late 1918: a new owner.

Majority shareholder and team president Charles "Lucky Charlie" Weeghman had spent wildly in his early days at the helm by purchasing the likes of pitchers Grover Alexander and Lefty Tyler, but as his business luck soured and attendance lagged during the war, he slowly began selling off shares of his stock to minority investor William Wrigley, Jr. On November 19, 1918, just eight days after the armistice was signed to end the fighting in Europe, saving baseball from a possible shutdown in the process, Weeghman announced he was stepping down as president of the National League champions. By mid-1920, "Lucky Charlie" would declare bankruptcy.

Manager Fred Mitchell took Weeghman's "president" title briefly, but the organization's chief decision-maker was clearly its new majority owner: Wrigley. A Philadelphia native, he had broken off from his family's soap manufacturing business and moved to Chicago in the early 1890s, determined to make his own way. He discovered, however, that the baking powder he gave away as a "bonus" item with his soap was actually more popular with customers than the sudsy stuff. Shifting his focus to baking powder, he started giving away chewing gum as his premium. Once again, however, the gift outshined the primary product. Wrigley was soon concentrating on gum as his key commodity.

Introducing both the Wrigley's Spearmint and Juicy Fruit brands in 1893, Wrigley became the nation's foremost chewing gum magnate. Among Chicago's wealthiest businessmen by 1916, he was one of nine investors rounded up by Weeghman that January to purchase the Cubs. Now, less than three years later, Wrigley had become top man of the National League's top team. Success, it appeared, had a way of sticking to him.

Pictured below are, from left to right, Grover Alexander, William Wrigley, and Bill Killefer. Killefer helped the Cubs reach the 1918 World Series as a catcher, but while managing the club he could do no better than fourth. His mediocre career record of 300-293 from 1921 to '25 did not make people forget Frank Chance.

Alexander the Great

GROVER CLEVELAND ALEXANDER

GREAT NATIONAL LEAGUE PITCHER
FOR TWO DECADES WITH PHILLIES,
CUBS AND CARDINALS STARTING
IN 1911. WON 1926 WORLD CHAMPIONSHIP
FOR CARDINALS BY STRIKING OUT
LAZZERI WITH BASES FULL IN
FINAL CRISIS AT YANKEE STADIUM.

Befitting his place among baseball's all-time greats, Alexander was just the ninth player elected, in 1938, to the Hall of Fame, following Ty Cobb, Babe Ruth, Honus Wagner, Christy Mathewson, Walter Johnson, Napoleon Lajoie, Tris Speaker, and Cy Young. By the time he died in 1950, Alexander was nearly penniless.

As troubled as he was tremendous, Grover Cleveland Alexander stood out in 1919–25 as an elite future Hall of Famer atop a mostly forgettable Cubs roster. Few players were in the right-hander's class as a pitcher, and perhaps no star ever overcame greater physical and emotional hardships to maintain his skills.

Born in 1887 and named for the sitting U.S. president, Alexander was one of 13 children raised in a Nebraska farming community. Signed by the Phillies, Alexander notched 28 wins as a rookie in 1911, including seven shutouts. This would become an Alexander trademark. When the control artist was winning 31, 33, and 30 games between 1915 and '17, more than a third were by shutout—including a record 16 in 1916 alone. In two of these seasons he led the NL in wins, ERA, and strikeouts to capture pitching's Triple Crown.

The United States had entered World War I by 1917, and because Alexander was rumored as a likely draftee, he was traded to the Cubs prior to the '18 season (along with catcher Bill Killefer) for two lesser lights and a boatload of cash (around $60,000). He was indeed lost to the army most of that year, but he returned in 1919 to compile nine shutouts and a 1.72 ERA for the third-place Cubs. Both marks led the National League, and he followed them up with 27 wins—and his third Triple Crown—the next year.

Quick on the mound and with no wasted effort in his delivery, Alexander had a strong fastball and curve along with great control (once pitching 51 innings without allowing a walk). Making his skills all the more remarkable were the challenges he endured just to play. These included epilepsy, alcoholism, and deafness in his left ear brought on by the intense shelling he encountered on the European battlefront. He eventually lost the ear to cancer, and he was haunted by his wartime experiences.

By the time he was sold to the Cardinals in 1926 amid worsening alcoholism, Alexander had collected 128 of his 373 lifetime victories (tied for third all-time) in Chicago. He then promptly helped the Cards beat the Yankees with three stellar World Series appearances that fall. As one biographer aptly put it, Alexander "had difficulty with just about everything in life except pitching." On the mound was where he belonged.

A telephone lineman in his early years, Alexander would reach new heights as a pitcher. Ironically, both he and Giants great Christy Mathewson, who tied for third all-time with 373 victories apiece, had their lives severely impacted by their service during World War I.

Going Through the Motions— and the Managers

In 1906, an NL pennant had been the springboard to greatness for the Cubs; in 1918, it was simply a one-year respite from a long stretch of mediocrity. Chicago fell to third place in 1919—21 games behind champion Cincinnati. For six years after that they never got closer than 12 games to the top. Things bottomed out in the '25 season, when the Cubs went 68–86 and finished dead last in the National League for the first time in more than a quarter-century.

There were some high points. Pitcher Grover Alexander excelled in the rotation,

Fred Mitchell earned his Cubs managerial post after being a well-respected coach with Boston's "Miracle Braves" during their 1914 World Series run. After his four years in Chicago (308–269 with 5 ties), which also included a very short term as team president, he skippered the Braves and then coached Harvard College in his native Cambridge, Massachusetts.

never posting a losing record in his nine years with the club. Left-hander Hippo Vaughn also had a few more strong seasons on the mound, and first baseman Ray Grimes, centerfielder Jigger Statz, and third baseman Bernie Friberg were all solid performers. Young catcher Charles Leo "Gabby" Hartnett developed into a top-flight receiver by the mid-'20s, and shortstop Charlie Hollocher, when healthy, was one of the league's outstanding young hitters and fielders.

It wasn't enough. The problems varied; suspect pitching would mar one year, while the next would be lost in a slew of key injuries. The gambling accusations that hit the club in 1919 also didn't help, and managers struggled amid the challenges. After leading Chicago to a pennant in his second season as skipper (1918), Fred Mitchell could not keep the team in contention in either of the next two summers. Fired after the 1920 season, he was replaced by a hero from the past—Johnny Evers—who lasted less than a year before stepping down due to illness and ineffectiveness. Soft-spoken Bill Killefer, winding down his catching

Manager Bill Killefer (right) appears to be pointing something out to coach George Gibson. In mid-1925, Gibson would briefly get his own shot at doing the pointing when he replaced fired skipper Rabbit Maranville, who had himself replaced Killefer that same year. By the next spring, Gibson would be gone, too. Confused? So were Cubs fans.

career with the club, was next at the helm. He kept the club hovering in fourth and fifth place for four years, but then he was ousted in mid-1925 after a slide to last.

Killefer's successors, shortstop Rabbit Maranville and former catcher George Gibson, each lasted barely a month. Maranville was fired due to his lack of discipline with a flask. A true leader was needed, and he'd be found toiling in the minor leagues.

A Day at the Ballpark, 1925

Weeghman's Cubs had become Wrigley's Cubs, so it was only natural that the venue formerly known as Weeghman Park would in time take on a fresh name: Wrigley Field. The team's new owner (who also bought the park and property in '24) kept some of his predecessor's nicest innovations alive at the North Side locale, which a decade earlier had become the first big-league ballpark to have permanent concession stands and to allow fans to keep foul balls rather than throw them back. But he also made many more changes even before the name change in 1926.

Wrigley hired the park's original architect, Zachary Taylor Davis, to do a complete renovation after the 1922 season, including lowering the entire field three feet to improve fan sightlines and pulling back the stands behind home plate and in left field (using rollers) to make room for additional seats. Outfield bleachers were built the next year, and "official" capacity, which was often exceeded, grew from 14,000 to 20,000. To reach out to more well-heeled fans, Wrigley built additional box seats, although cheap bleacher ducats remained plentiful. Not everybody came to the park in their best suits anymore, but there were still plenty of ties, as well as more women and kids.

Whether they came by foot, streetcar, elevated train, or even car, visitors to the ballpark in '25 were seeing a first-class venue. The ballpark was repainted each year, and a new drainage system kept the grass a brilliant green.

If a patron missed some action while grabbing a hot dog (now the most popular ballpark food), he or she could glance out at the large scoreboard beyond the outfield stands for an update. A unique feature of this board was the baseball-playing "Doublemint Twins" atop it—characters familiar to spectators who enjoyed the owner's Doublemint chewing gum. And if they couldn't make it to the park at all, fans of the mid-'20s had an exciting new way to follow their Cubs: on the radio.

Top: One unique feature of the old scoreboard at Wrigley Field, which was taken down after the 1937 season, was the presence of the Wrigley's gum "Doublemint Twins" (or "stick men") playing baseball on top of it. Fans enjoyed them, and the owner got a free product plug. *Above:* In 1917, as now, Cubs fans could avoid traffic challenges around the ballpark by taking the elevated train to games. Today's discerning rider should take the Red Line to Addison or the Brown Line to Southport.

CHAPTER FOUR

THE SALAD DAYS: 1926–1938

STAR PLAYERS, BIG-NAME managers, and a revamped Wrigley Field all took center stage as the Cubs regained their form as perennial contenders and claimed four National League pennants in 10 years. A world championship eluded the club, but attendance at Wrigley reached record numbers.

Above: Gabby Hartnett was a very obliging autograph signer, which was especially important when the kid he was signing for was a friend of mobster Al Capone—and Big Al himself *(right)* was watching. After Commissioner Landis expressed his displeasure at such fraternization, Hartnett reportedly said, "If you don't want anybody to talk to the Big Guy, Judge, *you* tell him."
Opposite: The infield for the 1938 NL pennant-winning Cubs included starters *(left to right)* Ripper Collins at first base, Billy Herman at second, Bill Jurges at short, and Stan Hack at third. Hack and Herman, who would team together for 10 years, both started in the '38 All-Star Game.

Great Managers, Great Teams, Great Crowds

It was the fall of 1925, and the Cubs had just finished dead last in the National League for the first time in club history.

Team president Bill Veeck, Sr., who had gone through three managers during the previous summer seeking the right fit for his rambunctious roster, traveled to French Lick, Indiana, to meet with minor-league field boss Joe McCarthy. Those who had played for "Marse Joe" praised him as tough but fair, and he had just led his Louisville Colonels to the American Association title. Though McCarthy had never reached the majors as a player or coach, he had experience that dated back to when he was a 26-year-old second baseman in the New York State League during 1913. Veeck liked McCarthy's makeup, and on October 12, he gave the Germantown, Pennsylvania, native the job.

The move marked a break from the Cubs tradition of making managerial appointments from the team's current or past roster, and some veterans grumbled about the "busher" taking the helm. They soon changed their tune, however, as it signaled the start of the third great era in franchise history. Beginning with a leap to fourth place under McCarthy in 1926, the Cubs would finish in the first division for 13 consecutive years. Included in the string would be six 90-win seasons and four World Series appearances, as Marse Joe and successors Rogers Hornsby, Charlie Grimm, and Gabby Hartnett contended for the NL pennant on an almost annual basis.

Consistency and longevity were the standards for Chicago players during the era. Grimm, Hartnett, Stan Hack, Phil Cavarretta, and Charlie Root all began stellar careers of 15 years or more with the team, and they proved immensely popular performers who exuded class on and off the field. This put them in sharp contrast with a pair of Hall of Fame teammates from the period whose immense talents could not hide their shortcomings in discipline and decorum: Rogers Hornsby and Hack Wilson. Cantankerous yet colorful, this duo provided juicy headlines along with prodigious hitting while the rest went more quietly about their jobs.

Fellow future Cooperstown inductees Kiki Cuyler and Billy Herman also stopped in for several strong seasons, and even sore-armed Dizzy Dean—despite never coming close to

Second baseman Billy Herman excelled in the field and at the plate. Forming an outstanding double-play combination with shortstop Bill Jurges on three Cubs pennant-winning clubs, he also hit .325 or higher four times and was a doubles machine during his 1931–41 Chicago tenure. Named captain in 1936, he earned Cooperstown induction 39 years later.

WILLIAM JENNINGS HERMAN
CHICAGO, N. L.   BROOKLYN, N. L.
BOSTON, N. L.   PITTSBURGH, N. L.
1931 – 1947
MASTER OF HIT-AND-RUN PLAY OWNED .304 LIFETIME BATTING AVERAGE. MADE 200 OR MORE HITS IN SEASON THREE TIMES. LED LEAGUE IN HITS (227) AND DOUBLES (57) IN 1935. SET MAJOR LEAGUE RECORD FOR SECOND BASEMEN WITH FIVE SEASONS OF HANDLING 900 OR MORE CHANCES AND N.L. MARK OF 466 PUTOUTS IN 1933. LED LOOP KEYSTONERS IN PUTOUTS SEVEN TIMES.

Kiki Cuyler was an established star outfielder with the Pirates when a feud with manager Donie Bush led to his being benched and then traded to Chicago for two journeymen players after the 1927 season. Pittsburgh's loss was Chicago's gain, as Cuyler averaged .325 with power, speed, and brilliant fielding over the next seven-plus years.

The Cubs led the major leagues with 171 home runs in 1930, and according to Louisville Slugger it was all in the bats. Here *(from left)* Kiki Cuyler, Rogers Hornsby, Hack Wilson, Charlie Grimm, and Riggs Stephenson pose with their weapons of choice.

regaining the 30-win form he had enjoyed in St. Louis—offered occasional glimpses of his past brilliance. The convergence of talent made the Cubs one of baseball's strongest franchises. It also resulted in National League pennants in 1929, '32, '35, and '38 (although, alas, a World Series win in this stretch eluded them). Attendance at Wrigley Field soared to new heights. Just 622,610 fans had looked on during the last-place year of '25, but this number jumped to league-leading figures of 885,063 and then 1,159,168 over the next two years as McCarthy and the talented roster took hold. Chicago was the first National League club to draw one million. By 1929 and '30, nearly 1.5 million were pushing the Wrigley turnstiles, figures that

Cubs' Murderers Row
Slays them with Louisville Sluggers

LOUISVILLE SLUGGER
Bats

wouldn't be matched there for 40 years.

To accommodate this increase, the ballpark was extensively remodeled and enlarged, with a second deck, left-field bleachers, and a new scoreboard all added. Brick fences throughout and ivy on the outfield walls were further touches that provided a unique charm to the park at the corner of Clark and Addison. These touches are still intact today. And while the deaths of both Veeck and owner William Wrigley, Jr., in the early 1930s were sad moments in franchise history, Wrigley's son Philip, as the club's new president, was committed to ensuring that the standards of excellence both men had set were continued.

Shown warming up before his first Cubs start on April 20, 1938, Dizzy Dean proclaimed after his victory that "I'm going to win 30 this year, just to show some of these guys who said I was through." Acquired from the Cardinals for three players and $185,000, the sore-armed former 30-game winner would fall 23 short.

LIVE FROM WRIGLEY FIELD

Broadcast it, and they will come. While some major-league owners in the 1920s were reluctant to adopt radio out of fear that fans listening to games would stop coming to the ballpark, William Wrigley, Jr., correctly surmised that the medium would in fact pull in spectators excited by what they heard. "The more outlets, the better," he told players. "That way we'll tie up the entire city."

By the mid-'20s, five different stations were transmitting home games from Wrigley Field, and favorite "voices" emerged. There was Quin Ryan (also program manager at powerful WGN), comedian Joe E. Brown, and Russ Hodges, later a longtime Giants radio man. Topping them in popularity, writer Curt Smith estimated in his acclaimed book, *Voices of the Game*, was "paternal, reassuring Bob Elson, his voice an incubative monotone, who lauded sponsors and recited gin-rummy stories." Recipient of the Ford Frick Award in 1979, Elson also did White Sox games and was a Chicago baseball institution for more than 40 years.

Joe E. Brown

Russ Hodges

Bill Veeck, Sr., Builds a Winner

It's often been said that the best bosses are those who know how to delegate. If this is true, than the finest move William Wrigley, Jr., made during his 14 years as Cubs owner was undoubtedly appointing Bill Veeck, Sr., team president.

Having previously observed the Cubs from the other side as a sportswriter for the *Chicago American*, Veeck took his post with the team in 1919, when the Cubs had just captured the NL pennant. Veeck knew an overhaul was necessary. He was steady and smart, just the type of calm, uncontroversial leader needed by the club after some 15 turbulent years under "the three Charlies": Murphy, Thomas, and Weeghman. Veeck worked well with Wrigley, who usually took his advice on all baseball decisions. It was Veeck, for instance, who encouraged Wrigley to buy the Los Angeles Angels of the Pacific Coast League, a top minor-league franchise that would provide the Cubs with several strong ballplayers in the years to come. And when Wrigley purchased Santa Catalina Island off the California coast, Veeck oversaw construction of a stadium and other facilities on this unique spring training locale.

The most important decisions Veeck made, however, involved the roster. Acting as a modern-day general manager (a title not yet used), he acquired Hack Wilson, Kiki Cuyler, and Rogers Hornsby, all of whom helped return the team to prominence. He saw the virtues of minor-league manager Joe McCarthy and then was validated when McCarthy piloted the club to a pennant in 1929. Veeck also made two good moves involving Charlie Grimm. He first traded for the slick-fielding, .300-hitting first baseman following the 1924 season and then appointed him manager eight years later. Under Grimm, the Cubs captured their second NL title of the Veeck era in 1932.

Unfortunately, that would also be Veeck's last healthy season. He died at 56 of leukemia on October 5, 1933, less than two years after Wrigley's death. Appropriately, one of his final wishes was that the Cubs and White Sox not call off any City Series games upon his passing. Honoring this dedication as well as the successes the families had enjoyed together, Philip "P. K." Wrigley, William's son and heir as owner, gave Bill's 18-year-old son, Bill, Jr., an office boy job at $18 per week in 1935.

The brain trust of the Cubs from 1926 to 1930 was *(from left)* Joe McCarthy, William Wrigley, and Bill Veeck, Sr. This trio built a powerhouse club, but then all too suddenly they were gone; McCarthy was fired late in the 1930 season, and Wrigley and Veeck died in 1932 and '33, respectively.

Wrigley Field may feel like an oasis in the city of Chicago, but for 30 years the Cubs also had a real-life island to call home. In 1919, Wrigley had purchased mostly undeveloped Santa Catalina Island, 20 miles off the coast of Los Angeles. After he constructed a baseball diamond and facilities on-site, the team spent most spring trainings there from 1921 to '51.

Wrigley Transition:
From William to Philip

Like father, like son—to a point. William Wrigley, Jr., never won the world championship he sought as Cubs owner, but he rebuilt the team into a successful and immensely popular club during his tenure. When he died at his winter home in Phoenix, Arizona, from a heart ailment on January 26, 1932, the chewing gum magnate passed the ownership mantle down to his only son, 37-year-old Philip. "Wrigley's Son to Carry on Dream of Winner" the *Chicago Tribune* announced two days later, and the headline would prove prophetic.

Philip Knight Wrigley (often called "P. K.") would indeed continue his father's pursuit of a

World Series title, and he would reach the fall classic three times in his first seven seasons as owner. The Cubs lost each of the showdowns to American League foes, but they remained highly competitive throughout the 1930s. While P. K. was carrying on his family's connection to the franchise, he was also carving out his own style of stewardship. William had been an enigmatic owner who spent rather freely in pursuit of victories, but his son was more conservative in his demeanor and with his checkbook—putting more of his money and attention into beautifying the ballpark and maximizing profits than beefing up the roster.

P. K. also didn't profess to loving baseball as his father did. William Wrigley's idea of paradise was his winters on Santa Catalina Island, which he had purchased and then outfitted with a stadium and facilities so the Cubs could spend spring training there. His son was happy to occasionally make it out to regular-season games at Wrigley Field. P. K. had no interest in serving as the club's president, and he only took the position begrudgingly after Bill Veeck's death in 1933 and the disastrous one-year term of William H. Walker that followed. "God knows, I don't want the job," P. K. said in '34. "If I could find another Bill Veeck, I'd put him in there in a minute, but he doesn't seem to be available. No matter who's in there, if anything goes wrong, I'm going to get blamed for it, so I might as well take the job myself."

He'd wind up holding the post 44 years, and the first several of them, at least, would be successful ones.

Chicago "Cubs"

7-William Wrigley-Owner

1-Joe McCarthy-Manager 4-Andrew Lotshaw-Trainer
2-Wm.Veeck - President 5-Grover Land ⎫
3-J.O.Seys - Vice Pres. 6-James Burke ⎭ Coach

8-Hornsby   11-Grimm   14-McMillan 17-Malone   20-Blair   23-Hartnett 26-Beck   29-Penner
9-Wilson   12-Cuyler   15-Taylor   18-Carlson   21-Blake   24-Root   27-Gonzales 30-Cvengros
10-Stephenson 13-English 16-Bush   19-Heathcote 22-Tolson   25-Nehf   28-Moore   31-Schulte   32-Grampp

COPYRIGHTED-1929
BURKE & KORETKE
CHICAGO

THIS HANDSOME PENNANT CELEBRATED THE FIRST CUBS PENNANT WINNERS SINCE 1918, FROM HORNSBY AND WILSON DOWN TO THE IMMORTAL HENRY GRAMPP (ONE GAME STARTED, ONE LOSS).

THIS MAGAZINE HIGHLIGHTED JOE MCCARTHY IN OCTOBER 1927 AS THE "MYSTERY MAN" WHO HAD TAKEN THE CUBS FROM LAST PLACE TO CONTENTION IN JUST TWO SEASONS.

Athletics rally in the ninth to beat Cubs

PHILADELPHIA, Oct. 14, 1929—Staging their second straight late-game comeback, the A's rallied from a two-run deficit in the bottom of the ninth inning at Shibe Park today to beat the Cubs 3–2 and capture their first World Series title in 16 years.

After the A's overcame an 8–0, seventh-inning deficit in Game 4 yesterday, home fans eagerly anticipated another rally as Philadelphia was stymied through 8⅓ innings by Cubs starter Pat Malone. Then they suddenly got it—with a single, homer, and double setting the stage for Bing Miller's title-clinching two-bagger off the scoreboard.

THE 1929 STOCK MARKET CRASH PLUMMETED MANY FAMILIES INTO DEBT, BUT COUNTLESS YOUNG CHICAGOANS STILL DREAMED OF GETTING A ROGERS HORNSBY GLOVE THAT HOLIDAY SEASON.

CHARLES LEO (GABBY) HARTNETT
CHICAGO N.L. 1922 TO 1940
NEW YORK N.L. 1941
CAUGHT 100 OR MORE GAMES PER SEASON
FOR 12 YEARS, EIGHT IN SUCCESSION, 1930
TO 1937 FOR LEAGUE RECORD. SET MARK
FOR CONSECUTIVE CHANCES FOR CATCHER
WITHOUT ERROR, 452 IN 1933-34. HIGHEST
FIELDING AVERAGE FOR CATCHER IN 100 OR
MORE GAMES IN 7 SEASONS; MOST PUTOUTS
N.L. 7292; MOST CHANCES ACCEPTED N.L.
8546. LIFETIME BATTING AVERAGE .297.

NAMED TO THE HALL OF FAME TOGETHER IN 1955, GABBY HARTNETT AND RAY SCHALK OF THE WHITE SOX WERE JUST THE SIXTH AND SEVENTH CATCHERS SO HONORED.

IN CONTRAST TO WORLD SERIES PRESS PINS, WHICH FEW FANS COULD ACQUIRE, BUTTONS LIKE THIS ONE DEPICTING THE 1929 NL CHAMPS WERE MORE EASILY ACCESSIBLE.

THE 1929 CUBS HAD PLENTY OF STARS, INCLUDING KIKI CUYLER, ROGERS HORNSBY (WHO HIT .380), CHARLIE ROOT, AND HACK WILSON. THEY STILL COULDN'T BEST THE A'S IN THE WORLD SERIES.

STEREOVIEW PHOTOS WERE MOUNTED NEGATIVES THAT PROVIDED A THREE-DIMENSIONAL IMAGE WHEN VIEWED THROUGH A STEREOGRAPHIC VIEWER. THIS EXAMPLE DEPICTS THE CUBS DUGOUT DURING THE 1929 WORLD SERIES.

Four Titles, Four Titans: Chicago's Managerial Heyday

Gabby Hartnett's 1935 season was one of his best. In addition to his usual great defensive work, the Cubs catcher batted .344 and drove in 91 runs in just 116 games. He then hit .292 with a home run against. Detroit in the World Series.

The Cubs claimed four pennants between 1929 and 1938, and the four men responsible for leading those championship teams were all unique personalities who left a large imprint on baseball history.

Before his hiring in Chicago for the 1926 season, Joe McCarthy had been a career minor-leaguer as a second baseman and manager. Despite McCarthy's lack of big-league seasoning, Cubs President Bill Veeck, Sr., believed "Marse Joe" could shake things up on his last-place club. It didn't take him long. In his first month at the helm, McCarthy had a locker room shouting match with ace pitcher Grover Cleveland Alexander and soon thereafter waived the popular but problematic hurler for broken curfews and drunken escapades. Alexander went on to help the Cardinals win the World Series, but McCarthy had made his point: He was boss.

Perhaps due to his own modest career, Joe had a knack for getting the most out of ballplayers. The Cubs jumped from last place to fourth in '26, and three years later they reached the World Series. Unfortunately,

In 1932, Rogers Hornsby (center) was the biggest star to ever wear a Cubs uniform, although he was often injured after his spectacular 1929 season. He could always hit, but by '32 he was a player-manager who almost never played.

personality that earned him the nickname "Jolly Cholly" and endeared him to players and fans. It also translated into victories, as Grimm claimed pennants in 1932 and '35. By mid-1938, however, the squad had fallen back to third when owner P. K. Wrigley sacked Jolly Cholly (other accounts say Grimm stepped down) in favor of another star player: catcher Gabby Hartnett. Gabby was no mastermind as a skipper, but he was smart enough to keep his own bat in the lineup. In '38, that move helped result in another title—the team's second of the decade to be won by two different managers.

Left: Joe McCarthy's philosophy was encapsulated in the "10 Commandments for Success in Baseball" that he created and taught. They were: 1. Nobody ever became a ballplayer by walking after a ball. 2. You will never become a .300 hitter unless you take the bat off your shoulder. 3. An outfielder who throws in back of a runner is locking the barn after the horse is stolen. 4. Keep your head up and you may not have to keep it down. 5. When you start to slide, SLIDE. He who changes his mind may have to change a good leg for a bad one. 6. Do not alibi on bad hops. Anyone can field the good ones. 7. Always run them out. You never can tell. 8. Do not quit. 9. Try not to find too much fault with the umpires. You cannot expect them to be as perfect as you are. 10. A pitcher who hasn't control hasn't anything.

a surprisingly one-sided series defeat to the Philadelphia Athletics and a failure to get along with team superstar Rogers Hornsby—who not so privately called him a "busher"—would cost McCarthy his job a year later. His successor was none other than Hornsby himself, who was as brash and domineering as Joe had been thoughtful and (usually) patient. Hornsby's myriad strengths as a ballplayer were not enough to make up for his inadequacies as a leader, and the team failed to jell.

Fired in mid-1932 with the club in second, Hornsby gave way to Charlie Grimm, a popular first baseman for the Cubs starting in 1925. Grimm couldn't have been more different than Hornsby, with a fun-loving

WORLD SERIES HEARTBREAK, 1932: THE CALLED SHOT

Babe Ruth hit 15 home runs in World Series play, but only one is still talked about today: The Called Shot.

The Yankees and Cubs were squaring off in Game 3 of the '32 series at Wrigley Field when Ruth came to bat against Charlie Root in the fifth inning of a 4–4 game. Amid taunts from the Cubs dugout, the Babe took a strike, looked at the Cubs bench, and appeared to hold up one finger as if to say, "That's only one." He repeated the gesture with two fingers after taking Root's second pitch for another strike. Some in the crowd of 49,986 then remembered seeing Ruth point toward dead center field, after which he promptly nailed Root's next offering into the bleachers. Others recalled no such gesture or thought he was pointing again at his Cubs tormentors.

So did Ruth call his shot? The debate has raged ever since the Yanks won the game and finished their series sweep the next day. Only one reporter, Joe Williams of the Scripps Howard News Service, made note of it in his game story, but his "Ruth Calls Shot" headline got the myth machine cranking. Ruth switched his version of events depending on his mood, but Root's denial was firm. If Babe had done any such pointing, the pitcher quipped, he would have gone down with the next pitch.

Enter the Rajah

The key to Chicago's 1929 season actually occurred five months before Opening Day, with a transaction that electrified the city and nearly caused Cubs President Bill Veeck, Sr., to quit his job.

Coming off a 91-win, third-place finish in '28 (just four games behind pennant-winning St. Louis), team owner William Wrigley, Jr., was determined to make whatever moves necessary to put his club over the top. He, Veeck, and manager Joe McCarthy all felt another power hitter might do the trick, so Wrigley sent the impoverished Boston Braves a record $200,000—along with five players—to secure the services of NL batting champ Rogers Hornsby. The greatest offensive second baseman of all-time and probably the best right-handed hitter *period*, Hornsby was a supreme talent with a .358 lifetime average, second only to Ty Cobb. He was also, however, a supreme troublemaker. "The Rajah" had a reputation for clashing with teammates and management, and when Veeck found out that Wrigley had acquired the slugger without following their normal protocol of discussing all possible deals first, he was livid. Wrigley had to assure his top executive that he would never pull such a maneuver again, thereby avoiding Veeck's resignation.

Judging from the reaction in Chicago, however, Veeck was the only one upset about the deal. The outgoing players—pitchers Bruce Cunningham, Percy Jones, and Socks Siebold, second baseman Freddie Maguire, and backup catcher Lou Legett—were quickly forgotten as newspapers toasted Hornsby. One photo in the *Chicago Tribune* featured a portrait of the Rajah superimposed over city skyscrapers, beneath the headline "New Tower in Chicago's Skyline." Some 50,000 fans packed Wrigley Field on Opening Day 1929 to see the big man in action. While fans were disappointed when Hornsby went hitless in a 4–3 loss to the Pirates, he came through the next afternoon with a grand slam in a 13–2 win.

This was far more the norm for the remainder of the season. Hornsby was named MVP after hitting an astounding .380 with 39 homers, 47 doubles, 149 RBI, and an efficient (and NL-best) 156 runs in 156 games. The Cubs finished 98–54 to win the pennant by 10½ games over Pittsburgh. Wrigley, it turns out, had spent wisely after all.

Hornsby's career before coming to the Cubs in 1929 had been one of sustained excellence. In each of the previous nine seasons, he had reached 200 hits and 40 doubles six times, he had also driven in 90 runs on eight occasions (with as many as 152), and batted below .361 just once.

ROGERS HORNSBY
NATIONAL LEAGUE BATTING CHAMPION
7 YEARS–1920 TO 1925;1928. LIFETIME
BATTING AVERAGE .358 HIGHEST IN
NATIONAL LEAGUE HISTORY. HIT .424 IN
1924,20TH CENTURY MAJOR LEAGUE RECORD.
MANAGER 1926 WORLD CHAMPION ST. LOUIS
CARDINALS. MOST-VALUABLE-PLAYER
1925 AND 1929.

In the years since Hornsby's 1942 Hall of Fame selection, no one has come close to matching his lifetime batting mark—still the highest ever for a right-handed hitter. Between 1921 and '25, his average was .402. No other big-leaguer since Ted Williams in '41 has even hit .400 once.

Jolly Cholly to the Rescue

Rogers Hornsby's turbulent one-and-a-half-year reign as Cubs player-manager was proof that .358 hitters often have trouble leading mere mortals who can't produce at the same clip. Despite his prowess at the plate, many of the Rajah's players came to dislike him for his abrasive personality and lack of patience. His job was secure as long as owner William Wrigley, Jr., was around, but when Wrigley died in January 1932, Hornsby's safety net was gone.

The Cubs had finished a disappointing third in the Rajah's first full season at the helm the year before, but they got off to a fast 22–9 start in '32. The team then spent the next several months slogging along at a below-.500 pace, and rumors began spreading that the superstar skipper was mixed up with gamblers and bookmakers. (It didn't help that many of those he owed debts to were his own teammates.) This was the ammunition new owner P. K. Wrigley and team President Bill Veeck, Sr., needed. They fired Hornsby on August 2, despite the club's second-place standing, and they elevated standout first baseman Charlie Grimm to the managerial post.

A popular player with the Cubs beginning in 1925, the affable Grimm ("Jolly Cholly") was an instant success. The veteran team warmed to his supportive approach—a direct contrast to Hornsby's dictatorial style—and emerged from their long doldrums to once again string together victories. Just 53–46 when Grimm took over, they soon went on a 14-game winning streak and in one stretch took 20 of 22. Moving into first place on August 11, they never relinquished it, finishing with a 90–64 mark and a four-game edge on second-place Pittsburgh. All told, they played at a tidy .673 clip after the managerial switch.

There were some strong individual performances. Second baseman Billy Herman hit .314 and fielded brilliantly, and Lon Warneke led the NL in wins (22) and ERA (2.37). But most fans and sportswriters credited Grimm's leadership, .307 average, and 80 clutch RBI for the end result. How did his teammates feel about the change? The answer was clear when they voted their World Series bonus money: Hornsby was not granted even a half share.

Grimm speaks to his Cubs team, which responded with a fantastic stretch drive after he replaced Rogers Hornsby as manager in August 1932. Slightly over .500 when Jolly Cholly took over, they went 37–18 the rest of the way.

BURLEIGH GRIMES APPEARS TO BE PITCHING IN A STRANGE, OZ-LIKE FIELD ON THIS 1933 BASEBALL CARD. HE MIGHT HAVE WELCOMED THE CHANGE; IN REAL-LIFE PARKS, HE WAS 3-6 FOR THE CUBS THAT YEAR.

THE CUBS WENT 86-68 IN 1933, GOOD FOR JUST THIRD PLACE.

HAZEN SHIRLEY CUYLER
"KIKI"

PITTSBURGH N.L. 1921 TO 1927
CHICAGO N.L. 1928 TO 1935
CINCINNATI N.L. 1935 TO 1937
BROOKLYN N.L. 1938

LED N.L. IN STOLEN BASES 1926, 1928, 1929, 1930. BATTED .354 IN 1924, .357 IN 1925, .360 IN 1929, .355 IN 1930. LIFETIME TOTAL 2299 HITS, BATTING AVERAGE .321. NAMED TO ALL STAR TEAM IN 1925.

AS HIS 1968 HALL OF FAME PLAQUE ATTESTS, KIKI CUYLER WAS A RARITY IN HIS ERA—A STAR WHO SPENT SIX-PLUS YEARS WITH TWO TEAMS.

IF THIS FAN KEPT AN ACCURATE SCORE OF THIS 1933 GAME AGAINST PITTSBURGH, BILLY HERMAN HIT A HOMER IN THE SECOND INNING TO HELP THE CUBS GET THE WIN, BEATING THE PIRATES 9-2.

WHILE OPENING THIS COLLECTIBLE MATCHBOOK, CUBS FANS COULD LEARN KIKI CUYLER'S REAL FIRST NAME WAS HAZEN. NOT REVEALED WAS HIS MIDDLE NAME: SHIRLEY!

THE DIAMOND MATCH CO.

1933 was lost to his team for long periods, having broken bones in both his ankle and foot.

Outfielder. Bats and throws right-handed. Age 34, height 5' 10½ in. Home, Harrisville, Mich. "Kiki." Great outfielder, fast base runner and has a fine throw. Has a 12-year batting average of .330. Brilliant star.

HAZEN "KIKI" CUYLER
Chicago "Cubs"

IN AN EXAMPLE OF THE MAGAZINE "COVER JINX" THAT PREDATES SPORTS ILLUSTRATED, WILSON PLUMMETED FROM 191 RBI TO OBLIVION WITHIN MONTHS OF THIS 1931 APPEARANCE.

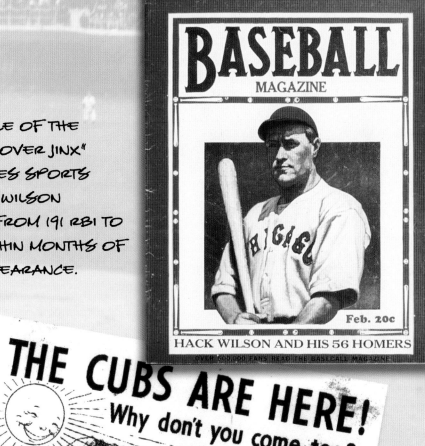

BASEBALL
MAGAZINE

Feb. 20c

HACK WILSON AND HIS 56 HOMERS

OVER 600,000 FANS READ THE BASEBALL MAGAZINE

Yankees notch third straight title with sweep of Cubs

NEW YORK, Oct. 9, 1938—The Yankee juggernaut continued to roll as New York finished off a sweep of the Chicago Cubs today, beating them 8–3, for their third consecutive World Series championship.

It was business as usual at Yankee Stadium, with the home club taking an early 3–0 lead against Chicago starter Bill Lee and adding four runs in the eighth after the Cubs crept to within 4–3. Shortstop Frankie Crosetti drove in four of New York's runs with a double and triple.

The Cubs have now fallen in four straight World Series since 1929, while the Yankees have won in their past six Series appearances since 1927.

THE CUBS ARE HERE!
Why don't you come too?

CHICAGO CUBS SPRING TRAINING TRIP- FEB. 21 - MAR. 12
SANTA CATALINA ISLAND

CUBS SPRING TRAINING WAS OFTEN HELD IN SANTA CATALINA, CALIFORNIA, FROM 1921 TO 1951. TOUR GROUPS WERE LED TO WATCH THE CUBS PLAY BALL—THE BEAUTIFUL WEATHER WAS A BONUS!

Cubs Hit Lucky 21

Right-hander Bill Lee was one of the key figures in Chicago's midyear rise from the doldrums to a pennant in 1935. The 6'3" curveball artist, known as "Big Bill" and "The General," went 20-6 and led the NL in winning percentage (.769) that summer, highlighted by his victory that clinched the pennant over the Cardinals.

Labor Day was founded to celebrate the achievements of American workers. In 1935, the Cubs marked the end-of-summer holiday by getting to work on the greatest title-winning push in baseball history.

After splitting a doubleheader with the Reds on September 2 (losing the second game), Chicago sat in third place, 2½ games behind the league-leading Cardinals. They had a day off, then beat the Phillies 8–2 on the fourth. Over the next 23 days, through an entire 20-game homestand and three more contests in St. Louis, the Cubs would not lose again. They captured tight games and blowouts, 21 straight in all, in an incredible streak highlighted by a pennant-clinching road victory over the Cards at Sportsman's Park on September 27. That was actually their 20th consecutive win; just for good measure, they then took the second game of that day's doubleheader for lucky 21. It was their 100th—and last—victory of the season.

How did they do it? A little of everything. Left fielder Augie Galan was the hero in the early going, driving in six runs in the win that started the streak.

He added two more RBI in ace Bill Lee's 4–0 shutout of the Phils on September 7—moving Chicago past the Giants into second place. A week later the Cubs took over first with a wild 18–14 win against the Dodgers, holding off a furious late-inning push by the Brooklynites. Right-hander Lee and lefty Larry French each won five times during the white-hot stretch. The league's best defensive infield—including Billy Herman at second, Bill Jurges at short, Phil Cavarretta at first, and league MVP Gabby Hartnett at catcher—kept miscues to a minimum.

Making things all the more exciting was that the Giants and especially the Cardinals also played well in September; they kept the Cubs from clinching until just three games remained in the season. In 1916, the Giants had won a record 26 straight but finished fourth. Though the Cubs streak was five games shorter, it still stands as the longest "meaningful" win streak of them all.

There are no poems to sing their praises, but Bill Jurges *(left)* and Billy Herman, here practicing their smooth double play, were a key to the Cubs' renaissance of 1929-38.

Hartnett's "Homer in the Gloamin'"

Proponents for installing lights at Wrigley Field may have eventually won out, but even they will admit that the park's most memorable moment would have been far less dramatic under the arcs.

The Cubs entered July 1938 in fourth place, five games behind the front-running Giants. When three more weeks passed and Chicago failed to make up much ground on New York or the surging Pirates, management decided a change was necessary. Accounts vary as to whether manager Charlie Grimm was fired or resigned, but in any case the team found itself with catcher Gabby Hartnett as the new skipper on July 20.

A rarity for the era, Hartnett would routinely don the mask 110-plus games a year while hitting for power and a high average. The Rhode Island-bred catcher had been with the club since 1922 and had been a bona fide star for more than a decade. His nickname, "Gabby," was earned through countless confabs with umpires and opponents while behind the plate, but the likable 37-year-old receiver quickly surprised those who thought this chatty fellow wasn't managerial timber. Just 45–36 when he took over, Chicago went 44–27 the rest of the season, including a 17–3-1 September stretch that set up a three-game showdown with the first-place Pirates at Wrigley Field. Winners in the opener (their eighth straight victory), the Cubs were just a half-game back with six to play.

The next afternoon, September 28, featured gray skies—the kind of day that would prompt a ballpark crew to put on the lights early. This was not an option, of course, so the teams played amid the darkening clouds until the Cubs batted in the last of the ninth. It was 5–5, and plate umpire George Barr had already declared the game would be called after that frame. Hartnett came up with two outs, and at precisely 5:37 P.M. he hit Mace Brown's two-strike curve into Wrigley's brand-new left-field bleachers. Although some in the crowd of 34,465 initially couldn't discern through the shadows that this was a game-winning homer, others were already on the field and blocking Gabby's path as he rounded second. He didn't mind. "I got the kind of feeling you get when the blood rushes to your head and you get dizzy," he said later. After a 10–1 thrashing of Pittsburgh the next day, he would also get another shot at a World Series title.

Tighter security at ballparks has eliminated scenes like this one—everyday fans joining Gabby Hartnett as he finishes running out his famous "Homer in the Gloamin'" on September 28, 1938. The identity of the man in the coat and tie has been lost to history, but he no doubt relished his inclusion in the famous photo.

Hack Wilson: Rum and Ribbies

His physique and expressions made him look almost cartoon-like at the plate, but Hack Wilson was very much a real-life threat to National League pitchers from 1926 to 1930, when he compiled 708 RBI in just 738 games.

He shot through the baseball universe like a short, squat comet, but Hack Wilson's legacy is assured by a single number: 191. While many of baseball's most legendary offensive records have fallen in recent years, nobody in seven decades has approached Wilson's standard for runs batted in.

Other figures can also be used to describe Wilson to those who never saw this human oddity in person. The average home run champ during the 1930s was around 6' and 190 pounds. Wilson, however, checked in at 5'6", 195 pounds with a barrel chest, a size 18 collar, and a size 6 shoe. One historian says Kirby Puckett was the modern player who most resembled him. Arthur Daley of *The New York Times* described Wilson as "built like two men sitting down . . . a giant hammered down to size, no neck and tremendous shoulders."

Lewis Robert Wilson, who likely got his nickname from a Russian weight lifter named George Hackenschmidt, was drafted by the Cubs in 1925 after the Giants left him unprotected in the minors. Inserted into Chicago's starting lineup, he promptly led the National League with 21, 30, and 31 homers from 1926 to 1928. His first monster year came in '29, when he had 39 homers and a league-leading 159 RBI.

All this was a warm-up for 1930. In a season when the NL league average was .303, Wilson batted .356 with the aforementioned 191 RBI in 155 contests. He also smashed 56 homers, the first man other than Babe Ruth to hit 50 and just four behind the Babe's legendary mark of 60. His NL dinger record stood for 68 years until topped by Mark McGwire and fellow Cub Sammy Sosa, and only Hank Greenberg (183) and Lou Gehrig (184) ever approached his RBI mark. Nobody has come within 25 of the total since 1937.

Unfortunately, Wilson loved rum as much as ribbies. This, combined with McCarthy's

departure and league measures taken to curtail offense in 1931, led to his numbers plummeting to .261, 13 homers, and 61 RBI. The dip made his drunkenness and clashes with new manager Rogers Hornsby, sportswriters, and even fans far more annoying. Wilson was traded after the season. Out of baseball by 1934, he died virtually penniless 14 years later.

Wilson's reign at the top of the National League did not last nearly as long as it might have had he taken care of himself. Until the wheels fell off, however, the Cubs slugger was constantly in the spotlight.

LEWIS ROBERT WILSON
"HACK"
NEW YORK N.L., CHICAGO N.L.,
BROOKLYN N.L., PHILADELPHIA N.L.,
1923 - 1934
ESTABLISHED MAJOR LEAGUE RECORD OF 190
RUNS BATTED IN AND NATIONAL LEAGUE HIGH
OF 56 HOMERS IN 1930. LED OR TIED FOR N.L.
HOMER TITLE FOUR TIMES. COMPILED LIFETIME
.307 BATTING AVERAGE AND DROVE IN 100 OR
MORE RUNS SIX YEARS. HIT TWO HOMERS IN
INNING IN 1925 AND THREE IN GAME IN 1930.

Like Sandy Koufax and Dizzy Dean, Wilson is in the Hall of Fame based on a short stretch of incredible production rather than a long, sustained career. But while it was injuries that did in Sandy and Dizzy, Hack's alcohol problems were seen as brought on by himself—one reason it took until 1979 for Cooperstown to recognize him.

Forget About the Babe—
This Guy Could Pitch

Charlie Root won at least 15 games eight times for the Cubs between 1926 and 1937, and he just missed on two other occasions. Seldom the staff's ace, he was dependable in any role—making 339 starts for Chicago and relieving in 266 other contests.

He won 201 games with the team, more than Fergie Jenkins, Three Finger Brown, or any other pitcher in Cubs history, yet he is mostly remembered today for just one throw in a 27-year pro career. Babe Ruth may or may not have "called his shot" before homering off Charlie Root in the 1932 World Series, but Root deserves more than that single moment as his epithet.

The Cubs team leader in victories, games (605), innings (1337⅓), and seasons as a pitcher (16) was born in Middletown, Ohio, in 1899. He came up to the majors with the St. Louis Browns in 1923. Just 0–4 in his first short big-league stint, he next spent two years with Los Angeles in the Pacific Coast League before coming back to the majors with the Cubs in '26. A stocky right-hander who worked extremely quickly, he was an instant hit in the rotation and easily topped the team's staff in wins (18), innings (271⅓), and complete games (21) during his first full season.

Were Cy Young Awards given back in 1927, Root certainly would have earned NL honors. Going 26–15 to lead the league in victories—no Chicago pitcher in either league has won as many since—he was also high man in games (48) and innings pitched (309) for the fourth-place Cubs. He never won 20 again, but he reached double figures on eight more occasions before becoming a valuable spot starter and reliever in his late 30s. Unfortunately, Root's one bugaboo was the World Series. He pitched in four of them for the Cubs and went 0–3 with a 6.75 ERA. In the infamous "Called Shot" game, he gave up a record four home runs: two each to Ruth and Lou Gehrig.

Still, Root was a major reason the Cubs reached those series, and in the regular season he was almost always reliable. He completed more than half of his 339 starts for Chicago, had a fine 42–26 mark with 40 saves out of the bullpen, and lasted at Wrigley until the 1941 season—never winning a game for another major-league team. He did, however, return to the minors at age 42 and win another bunch there before finally retiring at 49.

"Smiling Stan" Hack

It must have been frustrating to play in four World Series and never emerge victorious, but if it bothered Stan Hack nobody could tell. Possessor of perhaps the sunniest disposition seen at Wrigley Field in the pre-Ernie Banks era, "Smiling Stan" gave spectators and teammates plenty to grin about during his stellar 16-year career.

Tall and wiry at 6', 170 pounds, Hack was a California kid who got his start in the Pacific Coast League. A .352 hitter for his hometown Sacramento Solons in 1931, the 22-year-old gained the attention of Cubs owner William Wrigley, Jr. Soon thereafter, Hack had a Chicago contract. He saw limited big-league action the next two seasons, but by the second half of 1934 he was starting at third base for Charlie Grimm's squad.

Anything but a hack at the plate, Stan was a great contact hitter and leadoff man who walked twice as often as he struck out. He hit .282 or higher for 14 straight years en route to a .301 career mark. He never reached double figures in home runs but was good for 20 to 30 doubles a year and led the NL twice in stolen bases and hits. Seven times in his career, including a then-record six consecutive seasons from 1936 to '41, he scored at least 100 runs. A very strong defensive third baseman, Hack was rated the ninth-best ever at the position by baseball historian Bill James, just behind Hall of Famers Brooks Robinson and Paul Molitor (fellow Cub Ron Santo is ranked sixth).

Hack himself never made it to Cooperstown, and in fact he never received more than a handful of votes for election. But there were few players more popular in Chicago or the National League during the 1930s and '40s, and when it came to crunch time few were better. Stan hit .348 in 18 World Series games in 1932, '35, '38, and '45, but he was still waiting for a world championship flag to fly over Wrigley Field when he died in 1979. He even managed to keep smiling through three years as manager of the Cubs in the woeful mid-1950s, which in itself should be worthy of an award.

There was plenty for "Smiling Stan" Hack to grin about during his long (1932–47) career, at least during the regular season. Surprisingly, the immensely popular third baseman quit the team after the '43 season due to a dispute with manager Jimmie Wilson, but he returned once Wilson was fired in mid-1944.

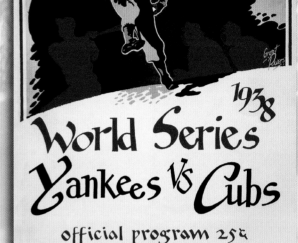

TRY TO BUY THESE
1936 AND 1937
SCORECARDS
TODAY, AND YOU'D
BE IN STICKER SHOCK—
THEY WOULD COST A FEW HUNDRED
DOLLARS AND PROBABLY EVEN MORE. IN THEIR
DAY, THOUGH, THEY ONLY COST 10 CENTS.

WHILE SIMPLE PAPER SCORECARDS WERE
STILL THE STANDARD AT BALLPARKS
DURING THE REGULAR SEASON, WORLD
SERIES PROGRAMS HAD BECOME GLOSSY
PUBLICATIONS BY THE LATE 1930S.

THE 1938 NL CHAMPS FEATURED
FOUR FUTURE HALL OF FAMERS:
DIZZY DEAN, GABBY HARNETT,
BILLY HERMAN, AND TONY LAZZERI.

GABBY HARTNETT WAS A CUB WORTH SALUTING DURING HIS LONG STINT AS A CHICAGO PLAYER AND MANAGER.

FANS DEPART YANKEE STADIUM AFTER GAME 3 OF THE '38 WORLD SERIES, A 5-2 YANKEES VICTORY. THE BRONX BOMBERS COMPLETED THEIR SWEEP OF THE CHICAGO CUBS THE NEXT DAY.

CHICAGO CUB NEWS WAS A HANDY INFO GUIDE FOR BASEBALL ENTHUSIASTS. THIS 1937 ISSUE SHOWCASED THE CUBS, BUT IT ALSO HAD STORIES ON DODGER BUDDY HASSETT AND MORRIS ARNOVICH OF THE PHILLIES.

Phil Cavarretta, Hometown Hero

Lou Gehrig in New York. Lou Boudreau in Cleveland. Cal Ripken in Baltimore. Every major-league city has its share of kids who grow up rooting for the local team, then starring for it. Phil Cavarretta's name may not be quite as well known as those listed above, but during the record 20 years he played for the Cubs, this native Chicagoan was revered as much as any of these Hall of Famers.

Cavarretta attended Lane Technical High School on Chicago's North Side, thus assuring he'd be a Wrigley Field devotee rather than a White Sox fan. He had a no-hitter and eight one-hitters as a high school pitcher, and he signed with the Cubs at age 17 before he even graduated. Upon getting his diploma in 1934, he was dispatched to minor-league Peoria and promptly homered in his first professional at-bat (he hit for the cycle in the same game). In September, while his former classmates were starting jobs or college, he was called up to the Cubs. He homered in his first Wrigley at-bat to give Chicago a 1–0 win on September 25. It was his first big-league hit.

After this auspicious beginning, Cavarretta's career took a while gathering steam. In 1935, he hit .275 at age 18 and succeeded manager Charlie Grimm as Chicago's starting first baseman, but he struggled over the next several seasons and missed most of the 1939 and '40 campaigns

with a pair of broken ankles (although he did hit .462 in the '38 World Series). An inner ear problem kept Cavarretta out of the service during World War II, and it was in this period that he most shined. He hit .321 with a league-high 197 hits in 1944, and then he helped lead the Cubs to the pennant with an MVP year in '45 that included 97 RBI and an NL-leading .355 average. Another great World Series (a team-high .423 average and 11 hits) followed, but it wasn't enough to bring a title to his fellow Chicagoans.

More strong years followed, and by the time Cavarretta ended his career with 77 games for his city's other team in 1954–55, he had collected nearly 2,000 hits and 900 RBI as a Cub while batting .293. He was far less successful as a Cubs manager from 1951 to '53, but by then nothing was going to sour the public on their hometown hero.

A terrific all-around player during 20 years with the Cubs, Chicago-bred Phil Cavarretta placed among the NL's top five at least once in batting, slugging, runs, runs batted in, doubles, triples, walks, and on-base percentage. Named MVP in 1945, he received votes for the award six other times.

A Day at the Ballpark, 1938

Beer and ivy came to Wrigley Field during the 1930s, and the ballpark has never been the same. The lifting of Prohibition had finally allowed for the sale of cold, sudsy ones at Cubs games in '33. With a championship-level team on the field, fans delighted in taking an afternoon to watch Jolly Cholly, Gabby, Smiling Stan, and the rest do battle.

It was a time of dramatic change at the corner of Clark and Addison. In 1926–27, William Wrigley, Jr., had added a second deck of outfield seats. Now, with the same fiscal enthusiasm his father had shown in acquiring star ballplayers, P. K. Wrigley used his early years as owner to embark on additional renovations that resulted in what broadcasters and fans took to calling "Beautiful Wrigley Field." The biggest changes came during the 1937 offseason and were supervised by 23-year-old Bill Veeck, Jr. New outfield stands and enlarged bleachers were built, boxes and grandstand seats were refashioned and moved to offer fans a better view of home plate, and a huge manually operated scoreboard was erected high behind the center field bleachers. Flags of National League teams were displayed atop the scoreboard in order of each day's standings, and an attractive brick wall surrounded fair territory.

Those arriving at games during the exciting 1938 season had plenty of other details to take in. Concession stands were better lit and offered more options, including the aforementioned beer as well as lemonade, hot dogs, cheese sandwiches, cotton candy, and Cracker Jack. The days of suits and billowy dresses were long gone, with casual shirts and slacks acceptable ballpark wear even for women. Ladies Days instituted by the elder Wrigley had done their job, and more members of the fairer sex than ever could now be seen, along with more children and teenagers. This had become a family ballpark with affordable prices: Box seats cost $2.00, and bleachers ranged from 25 to 50 cents.

Then, of course, there was the ivy. The wind from Lake Michigan had done in a small forest of plants and trees Veeck put in during 1937, so that September he headed up the planting along the outfield walls of 350 Japanese bittersweet plants and 200 pots of Boston ivy (ironic, considering that the locale most identified with the ballpark today is Boston's Fenway Park). The plants are long gone, but the ivy remains Wrigley Field's most distinguishing feature.

A bird's-eye view of Wrigley Field in 1938 shows the ballpark had already picked up many of the familiar features still seen today, including ivy on the outfield walls, a second deck, and packed stands.

CHAPTER FIVE

THE DOLDRUMS: 1939–1966

THE LONG, DRY spell at Wrigley Field began during this era, with just one pennant (1945) and three winning seasons between 1940 and 1966. Ernie Banks integrated the Cubs roster and outshined all players, black and white, but the supporting cast was thin as P. K. Wrigley's poor baseball acumen kept the franchise from rebounding.

Above: The '45 Cubs were a very balanced ballclub. They had the National League's best team batting average (.277), earned run average (2.98), and fielding percentage; the league MVP in Phil Cavarretta; and its hottest second-half pitcher in Hank Borowy. All they lacked, for their seventh postseason, was the ability to win four games in the World Series. *Right:* By 1947, when this shot at Wrigley Field was taken, the Cubs had quickly reverted to also-ran status—dropping from 98 to 69 wins in just two years. Big crowds were still common, however, and the team attendance mark of 1,364,039 was within 150,000 of the 1930 franchise record.

Wrigley's Wrongs and Other Blunders

Baseball marked its centennial in 1939, but Cubs players and fans were in no mood to celebrate. After an exciting pennant-winning rush the previous season, capped by player-manager Gabby Hartnett's "Homer in the Gloamin'," the team took a slide down to fourth place in '39 and was never really in the National League race. This marked the first time in 12 years the Cubs had finished lower than third, and it was a sour conclusion to a decade in which they had won four NL titles.

Hometown hero Phil Cavarretta was already a 10-year veteran by 1945 when the hustling first baseman took his game to a higher level. He led the league in batting (.355) while also notching 34 doubles, 10 triples, 97 RBI, and a league-best .449 on-base percentage. Named NL MVP, he added 11 hits and a .423 mark in the World Series.

Still, those looking on the bright side figured the club would soon be back in the hunt. After all, its 84–70 record was just five wins worse than that tallied by the '38 champs.

In the years to come, however, seeking bright spots at season's end would often be a challenging endeavor. If the period from 1926 to 1938 marked the third renaissance of Cubs baseball, the nearly three decades that followed were the Dark Ages at Wrigley Field. With the exception of a lone pennant in the summer of '45, when many of the game's top players were off fighting in World War II, the residents of Clark and Addison streets would *never* return to the World Series—nor would they even come close. Just how bad was it? Between 1940 and 1966, while Americans were electing five presidents and serving in three wars, the Cubs finished with a winning record just *three times in 27 seasons.*

As is often the case, fingers pointed upward in determining blame. In this case, that meant team owner and president Philip "P. K." Wrigley. An apathetic baseball fan at best—unlike his father and predecessor, William, who had understood and adored the game—P. K. was chastised for not taking proper measures to keep his club competitive as Phil Cavarretta, Stan Hack, Charlie Root,

Top: P. K. Wrigley didn't go to the ballpark as often as his father had, but he showed up to say hello to Gabby Hartnett during the exciting 1938 season. The owner's confidence in Hartnett was clear when he named the catcher to replace Charlie Grimm as manager that summer. *Above:* A highlight during another losing season in 1955 was the emergence of Ernie Banks, who became both the first big-league shortstop to hit 40 home runs in a season and—on September 19—the first player to hit five grand slams in one campaign.

and other stars of the '30s aged or retired. National League rivals such as the Cardinals and Dodgers built up tremendous farm systems that continuously produced strong young players, but the Cubs fell behind in this area. As a result, they had a far smaller nucleus from which to grow. When the Dodgers broke the color line by bringing up Jackie Robinson, the Cubs were slower than other clubs to follow, and this too set them back.

Wrigley's focus, his critics felt, was too frequently focused on the bottom line rather than the standings. He believed a clean, comfortable ballpark would keep fans happy and coming back, and he made major improvements to Wrigley Field while maintaining its charm. But you can't fill seats with a terrible team. At or near the top of the

NL in attendance through the 1930s and '40s, the Cubs fell off at the gate during the '50s and were dead last in this category by the time the 1962 club bottomed out with a 59–103 record—the worst in franchise history. At this time, Wrigley put into operation one of his oddest and most ill conceived notions, the "College of Coaches." But whether it was several "head coaches" running the team or a traditional manager, the end result was usually the same: a finish deep in the second division. Poor general managers including Jim Gallagher and Wid Matthews didn't help matters, and the cross-town rival White Sox—undergoing a revival in the 1950s—took over as top dogs in the city's baseball wars for more than a decade.

Some standout players did suit up for Mr. Wrigley during this long losing stretch, most notably the great Ernie Banks. By the time the self-absorbed but successful Leo Durocher was brought in as manager in '66, Ernie had been joined in the lineup by Billy Williams and Ron Santo, but contention still loomed far in the distance. Author Warren Brown's fine history of the Cubs, published in 1946, had concluded with a recount of the World Series just past and a mention that "they'll be back for more." He didn't state *when*, however, and 20 years later, fans in Wrigleyville were still waiting.

In 1959, no Cub other than Ernie Banks hit 15 home runs. The arrival of sweet-swinging Billy Williams *(left)* two years later would give Banks some much-needed support in the lineup and the franchise its first Rookie of the Year.

CUBS ON THE AIR: AT LEAST IT SOUNDED GOOD

Baseball and radio are a great mix—even if it's bad baseball. While the Cubs were losing through most of the 1940s, '50s, and early '60s, their fans could at least enjoy hearing some of the best radio and TV broadcasters in the business call the action.

Bert Wilson was the team's lead radio voice from 1944 to '55, and his familiar introduction of "Here we are at *beautiful* Wrigley Field," was given at the bequest of owner P. K. Wrigley before each home game. Wilson's other trademark call of "I don't care who wins, as long as it's the Cubs" became a frequent—and oft-unfulfilled—rallying cry.

Jack Brickhouse started on radio in 1941, and he later became the first "voice" for tele-

Jack Brickhouse

vised Cubs (and later White Sox) games broadcast by Chicago's WGN-TV. Fans enjoyed his style of letting the action speak for itself rather than talk over it, and his career lasted through 1981. In '83 he was named to the broadcasters' wing of the Baseball Hall of Fame, where many believe Jack Quinlan also belongs. An Illinois native like Brickhouse, Quinlan lent his smooth voice to Cubs games on WGN Radio from 1956 until his death in a car crash during spring training of 1965.

One Last Pennant

Most fans never saw it coming. The Cubs had compiled uninspiring records of 74–79 and 75–79 in 1943 and '44, and they entered the season of '45—the last to be marred by World War II—with much the same roster. Old favorite Charlie Grimm had returned as manager the year before, but even under Jolly Cholly the results had been deceptively decent; a fourth-place finish, but 30 games behind the pennant-winning St. Louis Cardinals.

In 1945, however, everything came together thanks to many strong performances and some help from Uncle Sam and the Yankees. The Cardinals, winners of the previous three NL titles, lost outfield stars Stan Musial and Dan Litwhiler and 17-game winner Max Lanier to the World War II draft, and their absence left room for the Cubs—with a far-less decimated lineup—to move up. At first Chicago didn't take advantage, hovering around .500 into mid-June, but then Grimm's troops took

Chicago's pennant-winning 1945 lineup included *(from left)* RF Bill Nicholson, CF Andy Pafko, 1B Phil Cavarretta, LF Peanuts Lowrey, 2B Don Johnson, and 3B Stan Hack. Other regulars included Lennie Merullo at short and Mickey Livingston at catcher.

On October 8, 1945, the Cubs beat the Tigers 8–7 in a wild 12-inning contest to capture Game 6 of the World Series at Wrigley Field. It turned out to be a win for the ages: Detroit took Game 7, and more than 60 years later the Cubs are still seeking a return trip to the fall classic.

off with a 35–11 stretch that put them in first place by early July. First baseman and hometown hero Phil Cavarretta was having a career season while outfielders Andy Pafko and Harry "Peanuts" Lowrey, both second-year men, appeared to be skipping right past their formative years to stardom. Veteran third baseman Stan Hack was also having a terrific campaign, and pitchers Hank Wyse and Claude Passeau led a surprisingly strong starting rotation. All told, the Cubs would have four men near or above 90 RBI and four pitchers with 13 or more wins.

Despite all these factors, the key to the season was undoubtedly the acquisition of right-handed ace Hank Borowy from the Yankees on July 27 (see sidebar). Borowy won his debut at Wrigley Field two days later and starred for the rest of the season as Chicago tried to fend off the Musial-less Cardinals. St. Louis players may have been right in claiming that they remained the NL's best team—they went 16–6 against the Cubs, after all—but when the two clubs met in late September for a two-game series at Wrigley, the Cards still needed a sweep to take over first. They got a split instead and went home for good a week later while the Cubs advanced to the World Series against Detroit with their tenth pennant of the 20th century.

The Quick—and Long—Drop-off

World War II did a number on the rosters of all 16 major-league teams as players were drafted or enlisted in the military, but by the time the Cubs met the Tigers in the 1945 World Series the war was over. Teams were returning to full strength. Unfortunately for the Cubs, who had been able to retain much of their starting lineup during the war due to various deferments, this meant the competition would be tougher than ever in their bid to repeat as National League champions.

In the end there wasn't much competition at all. The Cubs fell below .500 at the end of May in '46 and struggled to stay afloat in the NL pennant chase all summer. A brief flurry when they won 16 of 21 games in late August and early September got them within eight games of the Cardinals, who, with Stan Musial and other stars back, were atop the league once again. But Chicago couldn't keep up the momentum and finished third, 14½ games back. Blisters that severely reduced ace pitcher Hank Borowy's effectiveness were largely blamed for the 82–71 finish (a drop-off of 16 wins from 1945), but it was really more a matter of other teams getting stronger while the Cubs essentially stood still.

Fans still packed Wrigley in '46 and hoped for a quick revival, but the team's woes were just beginning. The Cubs dropped three more spots to sixth place in 1947 with a 69–85 mark, then finished dead last three of the next four years (with a lone "jump" of one spot to seventh in 1950). Aging stars Phil Cavarretta, Stan Hack, and Bill Nicholson moved on or retired, as did veteran pitchers Hank Wyse, Bill Lee, and Claude Passeau. Their successors—especially in the rotation— were not of equal caliber. MVPs Hank Sauer (in 1952) and Ernie Banks (in '58 and '59) shined individually, yet other than a 77–77 finish in '52, the team was below .500 every season of the decade. The '50s may have been fabulous elsewhere, but at Wrigley they were a dud.

Six years and one war removed from his playing days in Chicago, former Cubs second baseman/new Pirates manager Billy Herman reunited at Wrigley with his old infield teammates *(from left)* Stan Hack, Billy Jurges, and Phil Cavarretta on Opening Day 1947. Once the pleasantries were over, Herman's club won a 1–0 game.

He may have still resembled a skinny teenager, but Ernie Banks was well into his sixth full major-league season when he accepted his 1958 MVP Award from National League President Warren Giles on May 18, 1959. Ernie would duplicate the performance in '59—the first repeat MVP in NL history.

Bill Nicholson,
Wartime Homer King and More

There wasn't much to cheer about at Wrigley Field during World War II, but there was Bill Nicholson and his short reign atop the National League power charts.

A broad-shouldered yet athletic 6', 210-pounder from Maryland farm country, Nicholson had gone 0-for-12 with Connie Mack's 1936 Athletics in his first (brief) big-league trial. Banished to the minors, he was batting .334 for the Chattanooga Lookouts three summers later when the Cubs picked him up for a player to be named later and $35,000 of P. K. Wrigley's dough in mid-1939. He debuted in right field for the Cubs on August 1 of that year at Wrigley Field. He homered and then followed this up with two triples and a single in his second game. Soon the left-handed slugger was in the starting lineup to stay.

While he had joined the Cubs during the last of their 14-straight seasons in the first division, Nicholson still put up formidable numbers as the team struggled through the early 1940s. He was an All-Star in 1940 with 25 homers and 98 RBI, then nearly mirrored this performance in '41. Military service was not an option due to his color blindness, so "Swish" had to settle for becoming the top power hitter in the National League. By leading the Senior Circuit with 29 homers and 128 RBI in 1943, and again in '44 with 33 homers and 122 RBI, he achieved a

back-to-back feat no NL player—and only Babe Ruth and Jimmie Foxx in the AL— had ever previously attained. A strong fielder with deceptive speed for a big man, Nicholson finished third and second in MVP voting those two years, losing by just one vote to Marty Marion of St. Louis in 1944. In one doubleheader that year, he hit four home runs then was walked intentionally with the bases loaded by Giants manager Mel Ott.

Big Bill never reached those heights again, but he did have 88 RBI for Chicago's '45 pennant winners, plus eight more in the World Series. He also finished seventh in the NL with 26 homers in 1947, the eighth straight year he led the Cubs in circuit clouts. It would take Sammy Sosa to top that record, making it clear Nicholson was more than just a wartime wonder.

When it came to power hitting during 1943 and '44, Bill Nicholson was a one-man gang for the Cubs. In leading the league both years, "Swish" accounted for 29 of the club's 52 home runs in '43 and 33 of its 71 in '44. No other Cub hit more than eight either season.

Hank Sauer, the Tobacco Kid

By the time Hank Sauer picked up his 1952 MVP Award in '53, the Cubs were in the early stages of a big dip from the previous year's heady .500 finish. Hand injuries limited Sauer to a career-low 19 homers in 1953, but for a moment "The Mayor of Wrigley Field" could smile.

Time has not been kind to the legacy of Hank Sauer. One of the NL's top power hitters during the early 1950s, he is remembered today (when recalled at all) as a slow-footed slugger on a woeful Cubs team. Using his intricate "Win Shares" system, baseball historian Bill James has deemed Sauer's 1952 season the second weakest ever by an MVP winner.

Sauer was certainly no Willie Mays as an all-around outfielder, but this lack of respect seems a bit unfair for a guy who hit 288 career homers—all but seven of them after age 30. And despite what Mr. James has to say, collecting 121 RBI in a lineup where the next-best run-producer had 67 (and only two teammates were even over 35) is a valuable accomplishment. The home fans certainly appreciated it.

In a ritual repeated many times at the Friendly Confines, they would throw Hank pouches of his beloved chewing tobacco when he returned to his left-field post after hitting another homer. The legions there dubbed him "The Mayor of Wrigley Field."

Such adulation was a long time coming for Sauer. Originally signed by the Yankees in 1936, he was plucked by the Reds three years later in the minor-league draft. After a brief trial in the majors in '41 and '42, he spent two years in the service during World War II, sandwiched around four more seasons in the minors and another brief spell with the Reds. (Interestingly, his brother Ed saw time with the Cubs as a reserve outfielder during the war.) When Hank finally got a crack at more than 120 at-bats in Cincinnati, he set a team record with 35 home runs in 1948.

Not yet an offensively minded team, the Reds sent Sauer to the Cubs at the mid-season trade deadline on June 15, 1949, with Frank Baumholtz for Harry Walker and Peanuts Lowrey. It was a great deal for Chicago. Sauer hit 27 homers in just 96 games for the Cubs that year, then he smashed 32 and 30 the next two seasons before exploding for his 37-dinger, 121-ribbie MVP year. Multiple finger injuries slowed him in 1953, but he came back with a 41-homer campaign in '54. It wasn't enough to keep the Cubs from finishing seventh at 64–90, but where would they have been without him?

The White Sox "Steal" Back Chicago

In their battle for city supremacy, the Cubs couldn't have picked a worse time to have a bad decade. Just as the North Siders were plummeting into last place in the early 1950s, the White Sox were sparking an American League revival on Chicago's South Side.

The Sox had been poor cousins to their neighbors in terms of on-field success for most of the previous 30 years, a period in which the Cubs won five pennants and the White Sox zero. There was a wide gap in attendance as well, with the Cubs almost always on top, sometimes by as much as a 2-to-1 margin. Even in off years, the Cubs could use "Beautiful Wrigley Field" as a selling point, and they drew one million or more fans for six straight seasons from 1945 to '50. The White Sox, playing in less cozy Comiskey Park in a tougher part of town, had *never* drawn one million a season in a half century of existence through 1950.

All this changed in '51 when outfielder Orestes "Minnie" Minoso came to the White Sox in a trade. A .326 hitter that year and a defensive whiz, Minoso had great speed and 20-homer power. Along with two other emerging stars—lefty ace pitcher Billy Pierce and gritty second baseman Nellie Fox—he sparked the Sox to an 81–72 record, a 21-win improvement over 1950 and their best finish in eight years. The turnaround drew fans back to Comiskey. Attendance passed the magic million mark and stayed above it as other key players including shortstop Luis Aparicio, outfielder Jim Landis, and catcher Sherm Lollar joined the roster. Focusing on team speed and strong defense, the "Go-Go Sox" won 90-plus games four times during the decade, capped by a pennant in 1959.

The uninspiring Cubs, meanwhile, saw their fan base fall off along with their record. Attendance at Wrigley dropped below one million in 1951, briefly jumped back up the next year when Hank Sauer slugged the team to a deceptively optimistic 77–77 mark, and sank to 763,658 in the dreadful 65–89 summer of '53. It wouldn't rise back to seven digits again for 15 years.

The sight of Minnie Minoso scoring became a familiar one in Chicago during the 1950s, as more and more fans chose to see the fleet outfielder's exciting—and contending—White Sox team at Comiskey Park rather than watch the moribund Cubs at Wrigley.

By the time Minoso (left) was joined in 1956 by shortstop Luis Aparicio (right)— another slick-fielding, speedy performer— the White Sox were outdrawing the Cubs by nearly 30 percent. The gap worsened by '59, when the Sox won the AL pennant and their city rivals finished a 13th straight year in the second division.

GABBY HARTNETT PROVIDED KIDS WITH YET ANOTHER REASON TO EAT THEIR WHEATIES IN 1939: "YOU TOO CAN LEAD YOUR TEAM TO THE PENNANT!"

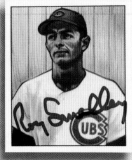

THESE HANDSOME 1950 BOWMAN BASEBALL CARDS DEPICT A TRIO OF STARS IN THE CUBS GALAXY; CAVARRETTA, PAFKO, AND SMALLEY COMBINED FOR 67 HOMERS THAT SEASON.

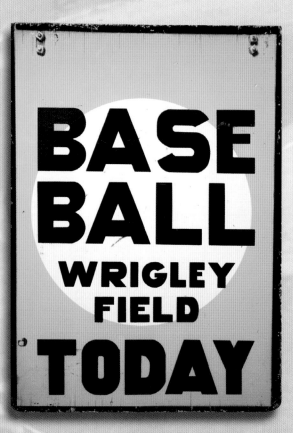

BASE BALL WRIGLEY FIELD TODAY

P. K. WRIGLEY'S ONGOING EFFORT TO MAINTAIN FAN INTEREST DURING THE LEAN DECADES INCLUDED APPEALING TO TRAIN PASSENGERS WITH SIGNS LIKE THIS ONE.

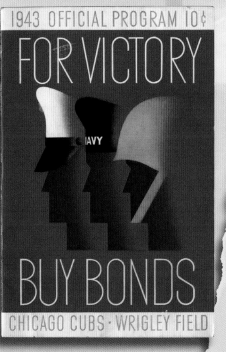

1943 OFFICIAL PROGRAM 10¢

FOR VICTORY

NAVY

BUY BONDS

CHICAGO CUBS · WRIGLEY FIELD

THE 1943 CUBS STRUGGLED TO A FIFTH-PLACE FINISH, WITH A 74–79 SEASON AND A .484 WINNING PERCENTAGE.

Tigers outlast Borowy, Cubs to claim series in seven

CHICAGO, Oct. 10, 1945—Hal Newhouser went the distance with 10 strikeouts and catcher Paul Richards had four RBI on two doubles as the Tigers beat the Cubs, 9–3, at Wrigley Field today to capture the World Series in seven games.

Chicago's starter was Hank Borowy, but the team's stretch-drive hero had nothing left after pitching in three previous series games—including yesterday's 12-inning thriller. Manager Charlie Grimm pulled Borowy after the first three batters singled, and reliever Paul Derringer could not stop the onslaught. Detroit led 5–0 after a half-inning, and Newhouser never let the Cubs get close while scattering ten hits. Chicago has now lost seven straight World Series dating to 1910.

HOW TO PLAY SECOND BASE

BILLY HERMAN
Chicago Cubs

BILLY HERMAN LED NL SECOND BASEMEN SEVEN TIMES IN PUTOUTS AND THREE TIMES IN ASSISTS, MAKING THIS 1941 BOOK A MUST-READ FOR ASPIRANTS TO THE POSITION.

THE HOMETOWN CUBS HAD JUST TWO PLAYERS SUIT UP FOR THE NL IN THE '47 MID-SUMMER CLASSIC: ANDY PAFKO (WHO SINGLED) AND PHIL CAVARRETTA.

ALL STAR SOUVENIR PROGRAM 25¢

WRIGLEY FIELD · CHICAGO 1947

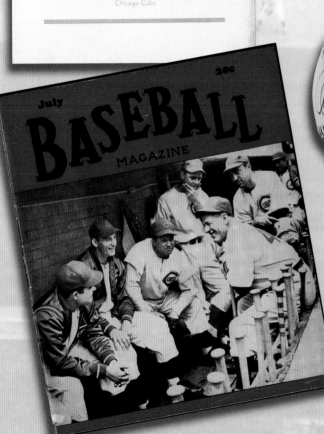

July
BASEBALL
MAGAZINE
20¢

ANDY PAFKO AUTOGRAPHED THIS BALL WITH THE CUBS' LAST WORLD SERIES OF '45; HE HAD TWO HITS IN CHICAGO'S THRILLING GAME 6 WIN.

ALL ★ STAR GAME CHICAGO CUBS 1947

THE 1947 ALL-STAR GAME WAS THE FIRST OF THREE HELD AT WRIGLEY FIELD. A WIND-SWEPT CROWD OF 41,123 SAW THE AL WIN, 2-1.

ON THE COVER OF THIS JULY 1944 MAGAZINE, CHARLIE GRIMM TALKS TO CUB PLAYERS IN THE DUGOUT AFTER HE IS REAPPOINTED SKIPPER.

"Mr. Cub" Arrives—and Thrives

Ernie Banks came to Chicago in September 1953, when Eisenhower was still new to the White House and African Americans were still relatively new to the National League. He helped integrate the Cubs roster, excelled with his glove and bat, and endeared himself to fans with a sunny disposition and strong work ethic. By the time he hit his 400th home run in September '65, the slim Dallas native with the powerful wrists had solidified his status as the most popular and talented player in the team's modern history.

The man known as "Mr. Cub" was one of the last great Negro League players to make the big leagues. A veteran of the Kansas City Monarchs, Banks was listed as age 22 when he debuted with the Cubs, but he was possibly as much as five years older. (Players shaving their ages to secure jobs was then common.) He hit .314 with two homers in his 10-game trial—he'd eventually play 424 straight contests to start his career, a major-league record—and the next year he placed second on the team with 79 RBI while smashing 19 homers as an "official" rookie.

From there Banks quickly rose to stardom, leading the majors in total home runs from 1955 to '60, while hitting 40 or more in five different seasons. He peaked with MVP honors in both '58 (when he hit .313 and led the league with 47 homers and 129 RBI) and '59 (45 homers and an NL-best 143 RBI). In the latter campaign he also set since-broken defensive records at shortstop with a .985 fielding percentage and just 12 errors. That year he became the first MVP elected from a losing team, a sign of the high regard in which voting sportswriters held him.

Knee and leg injuries that limited his range and some of his power prompted Banks to end another long streak of 717 consecutive games in June 1961. He then moved from short to first base the next spring. Soon he was the senior man in a top-notch infield featuring Ron Santo at third, Don Kessinger at short, and Glenn Beckert at second. Wrigley Field was ready for a revival.

ERNEST BANKS
"MR. CUB"
CHICAGO N. L., 1953-1971
HIT 512 CAREER HOMERS WITH MORE THAN 40 IN A SEASON FIVE TIMES. HAD RECORD FIVE GRAND-SLAMS IN 1955. FIRST TO BE ELECTED N. L. MOST VALUABLE PLAYER TWO SUCCESSIVE YEARS, 1958-59. LED LEAGUE IN HOME RUNS AND RUNS BATTED IN TWICE AND SLUGGING PCT. ONCE. ESTABLISHED RECORDS FOR MOST HOMERS IN SEASON BY SHORTSTOP (47 IN 1958) AND FOR FEWEST ERRORS (12) AND BEST FIELDING AVERAGE (.985) BY A SHORTSTOP IN 1959.

Banks's Hall of Fame plaque, which went up at Cooperstown after his landslide 1977 election, primarily cites his prodigious achievements as a shortstop. In actuality, he played more games (1,259 to 1,125) at first than at short after injuries prompted a mid-career shift. The Hall, however, recognizes him as a shortstop.

Banks and Baker
Blaze a Trail in Chicago

It had been another dismal summer at the corner of Clark and Addison. After showing signs of improvement in 1952 by reaching .500, the Cubs had fallen back deep below the break-even point the next year. By September of '53 they were battling to avoid seventh place when management announced it was bringing up two rookie shortstops.

Normally this wouldn't be big news in a woeful campaign, but these weren't just any first-year players. Ernie Banks and Gene Baker were the first two African American players in Cubs history. The team had actually purchased Baker's contract in 1950 from the Kansas City Monarchs of the Negro Leagues, and after four years of minor-league seasoning, his contract was taken over by the Cubs on August 31, 1953. Eight days later, Banks (who had taken Gene's old position with the Monarchs) was purchased as well, for one key reason beyond his .388 average: Baker needed a roommate. It had been six years since Jackie Robinson broke the major-league color line, but black and white teammates still did not usually share hotel rooms or receive equal accommodations on the road.

Once the duo donned Cubs uniforms, Banks saw action first, going 0-for-3 with an error in a 16–4 loss to the Phillies at Wrigley Field on September 17. Baker debuted three days later in St. Louis, in the same game that

Banks hit his first big-league homer. Once again Chicago lost, this time 11–6. And so it went. Although a 10-game winning streak just before the pair's arrival had helped save the team from the indignity of 100 defeats, this was still a club with plenty of holes.

For the next three seasons, while the Cubs kept struggling, Baker and Banks ably filled two of those gaps. Banks took over for the wild-throwing Roy Smalley at short, Baker moved to second, and the new double-play combination won over fans in racially tense Chicago. Both players had good range, and

while Banks possessed more power, Baker was also a solid hitter. Traded as part of a team-wide shake-up in early 1957, Baker later became a Pirates coach and scout and stayed friendly with his fellow pioneer. And when Banks made the Hall of Fame in 1977, the first person he called was Gene Baker.

When Monte Irvin *(right)* joined Hank Sauer *(left)* and Banks on the 1956 Cubs, it gave the club three sluggers who had driven in more than 115 runs in a season. Like Banks and Baker, Irvin started his pro career in the Negro Leagues; like Ernie, he'd make the Hall of Fame.

College of Coaches Is Graded an F

It may have been the craziest of P. K. Wrigley's moves as Cubs owner. After going through six managers in 12 seasons (including Charlie Grimm twice) while attempting to turn around his moribund club, the Cubs owner was sick of all the hiring and firing. Each time a new manager came on board, he wanted several of his own key coaches, which of course meant more firings.

Frustrated, Wrigley asked longtime Cubs coach Elvin Tappe for advice. Tappe suggested having a coaching corps that could stay with the team from one managerial regime to the next, half of them working with the big-league club and half in its farm system. This "brain trust" approach offered continuity and stability, but Wrigley wanted something a bit more unique. What if, he speculated, we did away with the manager altogether and let the coaches run the team on a rotating basis? Tappe may have seen the flaws in the plan from the start, but since P. K. paid his salary he went along with it.

The result was both ridiculous and disastrous. Wrigley's "College of Coaches" began in the spring of 1961, with the owner appointing a new "head coach" every month or so from among several coaches. As predicted, the shenanigans confused and frustrated players, as each boss of the hour sought to impart his own wisdom and make his own lineup and roster moves. The

experiment didn't help the team's record, either. The Cubs finished seventh with a 64–90 mark in '61 and ninth at 59–103 (setting a franchise record for losses) the next year. That was essentially it for the college. Although Bob Kennedy was called a "head coach" from 1963 to '65, he was never rotated out of his managerial role before moving to the front office in June of 1965.

"I don't think you will talk to one ballplayer who played under that system that's going to say anything different than it was *very* hurtful," Cubs pitcher Don Elston later said. Lou Brock, who believes the College of Coaches stunted his development and precipitated his infamous trade to the Cardinals, agreed: "I had two left feet, I was bewildered, and there was no one there to help. Trying to become acclimated to the big leagues, under that system, was the toughest thing for me in baseball."

They may be smiling here in early 1961, but by the end of Chicago's "College of Coaches" experiment two years later, the men who routinely traded off managerial duties for the Cubs during the '61 and '62 seasons would be bemoaning their part in the foolishness.

Buck O'Neil:
He Should Have Been First

During an incredible 70-year career in which he went from the segregated playing fields of the 1930s to becoming baseball's most beloved goodwill ambassador at the turn of the century, Buck O'Neil saw or accomplished just about everything possible in the game. In Cubs history, however, he'll be remembered both for what he did for the franchise and what it failed to do for him.

A smooth-fielding first baseman and two-time batting champ for the great Kansas City Monarchs of the Negro Leagues, O'Neil was too old at 36 to make it to the majors after Jackie Robinson broke the color line in 1947. He focused, instead, on helping younger African Americans get there, becoming manager of the Monarchs and preparing the likes of Elston Howard and Ernie Banks for big-league stardom. Next he was a scout, signing future Hall of Famers Banks and Lou Brock to Cubs contracts and tutoring a young Billy Williams in the minors before he, too, rocketed to greatness in Chicago.

The Cubs, to their credit, made O'Neil the first African American coach in big-league history in 1962, when segregation still thrived in the Deep South and Chicago's own racial tensions were high. But although Buck was in uniform from 1962 to '65 as part of P. K. Wrigley's "College of Coaches," he was never given an opportunity to manage the team or perform a visible on-field job such as

coaching first or third base. In one game, when that day's manager and third-base coach were both ejected, the pitching coach trotted in from the bullpen to coach third while O'Neil was left in the dugout. He called it his biggest disappointment in baseball.

O'Neil resurfaced and became an American icon in 1994 when his warm, insightful interviews highlighted Ken Burns's acclaimed PBS documentary *Baseball,* and the players he had helped never forgot him. Unfortunately, he died just shy of his 95th birthday in 2006 without ever being selected to join Brock, Banks, and Williams in the Hall of Fame, even by a special committee that inducted 17 other "black baseball" pioneers that very year. The huge outcry from people of all backgrounds, however, showed the progress made since he was left sitting on the bench. Love for Buck O'Neil had become truly color-blind.

Whether suiting up at the Polo Grounds (as he is here), other National League stops, or even home at Wrigley Field, O'Neil never got the chance to share his great baseball acumen as a manager or base coach, one of the great injustices in Cubs history.

CHICAGO CUBS

THE 1963 CUBS IMMORTALIZED ON THIS BASEBALL CARD WERE A REFRESHING 82-80, THE CLUB'S FIRST WINNING SEASON IN 17 YEARS.

KEN HUBBS, POSSESSING MATURITY AND INTENSITY BEYOND HIS YEARS, LOOKED DETERMINED TO CAPTURE 1962 ROOKIE OF THE YEAR HONORS—AND HE SUCCEEDED.

NEITHER ROOKIE ON THIS CARD FULFILLED THE PROMISE OF STARDOM, BUT OTHER CUBS NEWCOMERS OF THE MID-1960S (DON KESSINGER, GLENN BECKERT, KEN HOLTZMAN) WOULD.

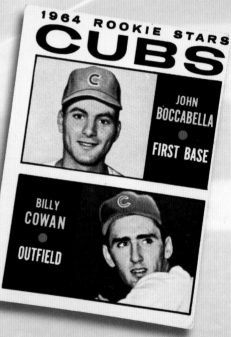

ERNIE BANKS'S AUTOGRAPH WAS IN HIGH DEMAND BY BASEBALL FANS IN THE 1950S AND '60S. CATCHING A BALL HIT BY MR. CUB WAS ALSO A POPULAR ACTIVITY. BETWEEN 1955 AND 1960, BANKS HIT 248 HOME RUNS, MORE THAN ANYBODY IN BASEBALL INCLUDING WILLIE MAYS, MICKEY MANTLE, AND HENRY AARON.

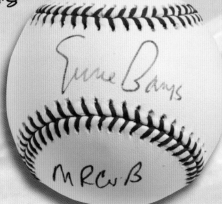

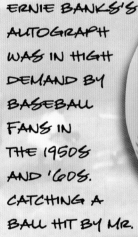

BEFORE HE WAS "THE RIFLEMAN" OF TV FAME, ATHLETE-TURNED-ACTOR CHUCK CONNORS WAS A .239-HITTING FIRST BASEMAN FOR THE '51 CUBS. HIS CAREER SWITCH WAS A GOOD ONE.

THE DISMAL CUBS OF THE EARLY 1960S MIGHT HAVE CONSIDERED SIGNING AGING ROGERS HORNSBY, BUT CHICAGO MAYOR RICHARD DALEY'S CATCHING FORM WAS STRICTLY BUSH LEAGUE.

Koufax is perfect, Hendley nearly so, in 1–0 Dodgers win

LOS ANGELES, Sept. 9. 1965—Sandy Koufax tossed a perfect game with 14 strikeouts in topping the Cubs 1–0 tonight at Dodger Stadium, but the great lefty's record fourth career no-hitter was nearly matched by Chicago starter Bob Hendley.

Hendley, a fellow left-hander with two wins to Koufax's 21 entering the contest, allowed just one hit himself—a bloop double by Lou Johnson—and gave up his only run in the fifth when Johnson walked, was sacrificed to second, stole third, and then scored on catcher Chris Krug's wild throw. "Don't forget the other fellow did a pretty good job out there," the classy Koufax said afterward. "We were lucky to get the run we did."

THE BACK OF THIS REISSUE OF THE 1954 TOPPS CARD NOTED THAT CHICAGO'S ROOKIE SHORTSTOP "LOOKED LIKE A REAL HOT PROSPECT FOR A REGULAR BRUIN INFIELD BERTH THIS SEASON."

ERNIE BANKS
shortstop CHICAGO CUBS

Wrigley Field Edition 2002

PHIL CAVARRETTA
CHICAGO CUBS

AS A CUBS PLAYER, PHIL CAVARRETTA WAS ALMOST ALWAYS SUCCESSFUL. AS A MANAGER, IT WAS ANOTHER STORY. IN HIS LAST SEASON, 1953, THE CLUB WENT 65–89.

Ken Hubbs, Shooting Star

The Cubs are counting on the 22-year-old phenom to solve their second base problems for years to come. The subject of this *Chicago Tribune* photo caption from July 1963 was Ken Hubbs, who the previous year had set major-league records for second basemen by playing 78 consecutive games and handling 418 chances without an error. He became the first rookie ever to win a Gold Glove Award, and because he was only 21 when the photo caption appeared, logic stated that the Cubs really could count on him for "years to come."

Whatever his age, Hubbs seemed suited for fame. At age 12, he had pitched and slugged his Colton, California, team to the Little League World Series title game, and in high school he was a four-sport star and student body president. Named National League Rookie of the Year by a landslide in '62, he appeared in 160 of Chicago's 162 games that season. In addition to his slick glovework, he batted .260 with 9 triples and 90 runs scored. The next season, although Hubbs's average fell off to .235, manager Bob Kennedy credited the sandy-haired second baseman as the anchor of an infield that helped the Cubs to their first winning record (82–80) in 17 years.

Teammates liked the tall, modest Californian who didn't drink or swear but joined them at bars with a smile on his face. According to his roommate, third baseman Ron Santo, Ken only had one problem as a rookie: a fear of flying. The next year, on

the plane back to Chicago after spring training, Santo says Hubbs surprised him by whipping out a pilot's license he had quietly attained during the exhibition season. "When I get up there, Ron, and I fly, it's like being next to God," Santo recalls him saying.

Family and loved ones sought comfort in such thoughts in the days after February 13, 1964, when the single-engine Cessna plane Hubbs was piloting crashed on a frozen lake near Provo, Utah, killing Ken and his lifelong friend Dennis Dayle. Santo and five other Cubs served as pallbearers at their teammate's funeral, and a Ken Hubbs Award was established to be given each year to the Cubs player who best displays "excellence and exemplary conduct on and off the field."

Top: On August 14, 1962, Hubbs signed autographs with the same steady right hand that had just helped the rookie set a new NL record with 57 consecutive errorless games at second base. *Bottom:* Cubs teammates and coaches served as pallbearers at Hubbs's February 1964 funeral in Colton, California. Two weeks earlier, in writing out his top ten goals for the '64 season, Ken had shown his selfless nature by putting "Win National League" at No. 1 ahead of "Bat .280," "90 RBI," and "18 home runs."

Say It Ain't So: Brock for Broglio

Three times between 1964 and 1968, Cubs fans were reminded of the club's worst-ever trade when they watched Brock star for the Cardinals in the World Series. Here he bats in Game 1 of the '67 fall classic against the Red Sox. Overall, he hit .391 with 14 stolen bases in 21 World Series games.

For Cubs fans of a certain age, three words still sting all these decades later: "Brock for Broglio." Perhaps no trade better symbolizes the dubious management decisions made by owner P. K. Wrigley and his minions in the years after the team's last pennant-winning season of 1945. When the Cubs at last emerged as contenders in the late '60s, diehards no doubt believe it was the ramifications of this deal that kept them from going all the way.

It looked like a bad move from the day it was made, but on June 15, 1964, it was actually Cardinals fans doing most of the griping. Ernie Broglio was a big, strong right-hander who had gone 18–8 for the Cards the previous season and 21–9 in 1960. He had started out just 3–5 in '64, but his ERA was still a respectable 3.50. At age 28, he was assumed to be entering his prime. Lou Brock of the Cubs, while blessed with tremendous speed, was a mistake-prone outfielder who struck out too much and couldn't hit for power or average. The 25-year-old had managed just nine homers in each of his first two full big-league seasons and was batting .251 at the time of the deal. Other names in the trade—Jack Spring and Paul Toth of the Cubs, Doug Clemens and a washed-up Bobby Shantz of St. Louis—were essentially throw-ins.

What transpired next was heart-wrenching for Wrigleyville patrons. Brock struck out on three pitches in his first St. Louis at-bat, but he then quickly emerged as one of the hottest hitters and best leadoff men in the National League. In 103 games for his new club, he batted .348 with 21 doubles, 33 stolen bases, and 81 runs scored as the Cards rallied to win the pennant and then the World Series over the Yankees. This was just the beginning. By the time he hung up his cleats in 1979, Brock would record 3,023 hits and a then-record 938 steals en route to Cooperstown.

Broglio? He took a month to post his first win for the Cubs and went just 7–19 with a 5.40 ERA over parts of three years with Chicago. He was out of the major leagues by the time Brock led the Cardinals to two more pennants and a second World Series title in 1967.

Broglio won this August 2, 1964, game for the Cubs, 3–1, but few others in his dismal three-year stay with the club. All told, the sore-armed former 20-game winner had just four victories in 16 starts for Chicago in '64.

Leo the Lip
Starts Righting the Ship

Durocher was all smiles when he took the Cubs helm in 1966, and he maintained his rosy outlook even as the club struggled through most of his first season. His attitude started to rub off in August and September, when the club went a promising 27–30.

After four years of aggravating players and fans alike with his absurd "College of Coaches," P. K. Wrigley took a dramatic shift by hiring Leo Durocher to manage the Cubs for the 1966 season. It would prove one of Wrigley's best decisions in more than four decades as owner, but its benefits were not immediately realized.

The cocky, combative Durocher, who had been a scrappy shortstop on great Yankees and Cardinals teams and later won three pennants and a World Series managing the Dodgers and Giants, was a still-spry 60-year-old who immediately declared that "This is not an eighth place club." The Cubs then went out and proved him right by finishing tenth—dead last—with a 59–103 record that matched the 1962 team for the worst in club annals.

Amid the losing, however, there were reasons for optimism. The '66 lineup featured several young veterans who were emerging as among the best at their positions in the National League, including third baseman Ron Santo (who had a club-record 28-game hitting streak during the season), outfielder Billy Williams, and second baseman Glenn Beckert. A trade brought in 23-year-old catcher Randy Hundley, who proved a fantastic defensive receiver and a solid hitter. Don Kessinger was coming along at shortstop, and Ernie Banks, though no longer a 40-homer threat, was still a clutch performer whose mere presence gave the team more legitimacy and class.

The Cubs could clearly hit, and their defense was steady with Santo and Hundley standing out. Pitching was a bigger challenge, but here Durocher encouraged the front office to take some short-term lumps to build for the future. Aging veteran hurler Lindy McDaniel was sent to the Giants in a trade that brought in the much younger Bill Hands. Two more starters whose best days were behind them, Larry Jackson and Bob Buhl, went to Philadelphia for young Canadian right-hander Ferguson Jenkins. By year's end Jenkins was in the starting rotation, as were Hands and rookie lefty Ken Holtzman. None managed a winning record, but all showed promise.

By September, with the Cubs playing nearly .500 ball for the second straight month, Durocher was telling sportswriters, "We're on our way up." Not even the most optimistic scribe or fan, however, would guess how fast that trip would be.

A Day at the Ballpark, 1957

The Cubs compiled a woeful .437 winning percentage during the 1950s, but their ballpark remained as cozy and appealing as ever, which is just the way owner P. K. Wrigley wanted it. In keeping the park in top shape and having his broadcasters extol the virtues of "Beautiful Wrigley Field," he hoped to shift attention away from his dismal team.

It didn't always work. Attendance at the North Side facility plummeted during the '50s and early '60s. The year 1957 was no exception, as the Cubs ranked seventh of eight National League clubs and averaged just more than 8,700 fans at home. Wrigley was the lone NL ballpark without lights, and this plus the fact that WGN-TV broadcast all 77 home contests may have impacted crowd size. Yet another deterrent was the neighborhood surrounding the park, which had declined somewhat. As the residents who had lived there since the turn of the century became wealthier, they began leaving for the suburbs.

Despite these challenges, Wrigley was still a wonderful place to watch a ballgame. The vines planted in 1937 covered the outfield wall, and the fans seated in the bleachers behind them were among baseball's most passionate rooters. The "Bleacher Bums" would not make their official appearance for another decade, but the "Bleacher Choir" was on hand to sing during the seventh-inning stretch and drink during the rest of the game. Ballpark attire was more casual than ever, with T-shirts and jeans much more commonplace. The afternoon starting times ensured there would always be plenty of teenagers and families on hand.

Bleacher seats cost just $1, while reserved grandstand seats topped out at $2, and box seats went up to $3. Even though crowds rarely scooped them all up, more than 20,000 reserved seats were made available only on game days, a practice that lasted into the 1980s and gave ordinary folks a chance to see big games if they were willing to stand in line. Once inside, fans in '57 could enjoy ice cream and bottled beer or take a ride to the upper decks on a series of motorized walkways. Unfortunately, the machines often broke down, and they were taken out in 1960. In this way, alas, they mirrored the product on the field.

Though those in the bleachers and cheaper seats may have dressed more casually in the 1950s to watch a game at Wrigley Field, most people in field box seats still dressed more formally.

CHAPTER SIX

REVIVAL AT WRIGLEY: 1967–1981

THE CUBS UNDERWENT a resurgence on the field and at the gate under fiery manager Leo Durocher, but late-season tailspins spelled their doom—never more so than in 1969. Departing stars Banks, Williams, and Santo gave way to some talented newcomers, but the wins stopped once Durocher departed the premises.

For a reason that has escaped baseball fans, Cubs team pictures in the 1960s and '70s often appeared in this "heads only" format rather than as standard photos. The difference did little to help the club's fortunes; this '76 bunch, for instance, went 75–87.

Ron Santo, Don Kessinger, Glenn Beckert, and Ernie Banks enjoy a laugh before a game in 1969. Unfortunately, the laughs didn't last. A late-season slide resulted in the Mets going to the postseason while the Cubs players watched the action on TV.

Leo's Legions on the Rise

Leo Durocher's mantra as a manager was "I come to win," and he surely had this in mind as his first Cubs team struggled through a miserable tenth-place finish in 1966. He had convinced owner P. K. Wrigley and general manager John Holland to trade veterans for young players, and as the newcomers settled in and took 103 losses worth of lumps in '66, Leo began preaching the same philosophy that had earned him pennants with the Dodgers and Giants.

"I've got to get these guys to believe in themselves," pitcher Fergie Jenkins, one of the new recruits that year, would recall Durocher telling him. "It's going to take more than a year. First they have to start believing that they can win. Then they have to go out on the field knowing that they're going to win, that they're the better club on the field. What has been beating this club is simple—stupid mistakes and lack of confidence."

It was hard not to agree with Durocher's

assessment. For years Chicago had the nucleus of a strong team in everyday stars Ernie Banks, Ron Santo, and Billy Williams, as well as experienced pitchers including Larry Jackson and Bob Buhl. Since 1960, however, this group had never risen above seventh place, and as Jackson, Buhl, and others were sent packing, the veterans left behind could feel a new energy taking hold. For the first time in a generation, it seemed, the Cubs were really focused on *winning* rather than just keeping the fans at Wrigley Field comfortable and happy.

It wouldn't take long for the secret to get out. The Cubs were the surprise team of the National League in 1967, reaching a high-water mark of 46–29 and first place on July 3. Jenkins, Bill Hands, and Rich Nye anchored a strong young pitching staff, while on offense the reliable Santo and Williams continued to do their thing. The youngsters—catcher Randy Hundley, shortstop Don Kessinger, and second baseman Glenn Beckert—showed the makings of All-Stars. Even aging first baseman Ernie Banks, the team legend and fan favorite whom Durocher had been hoping to replace, produced a first half-season worthy of a man ten years his junior. Defense and mental errors were improved, as Durocher had promised.

People throughout baseball raved about the action and attitude shift underway at Wrigley, including Mets coach Yogi Berra, who said the new-look Cubs reminded him

Top: Durocher and the Cubs acquired former Yankee free spirit Joe Pepitone in July 1970, and "Pepi" delivered 44 RBI in 56 games. The next two years, however, the flashy outfielder missed more than 120 contests due to injuries and irked Durocher with habits such as showing up at Wrigley in a limo. By early '73, Pepitone was exiled to Atlanta. *Above:* Rookie catcher Jody Davis and the Cubs were down and out in sixth place during 1981, but that summer's sale of the club by the Wrigley family to the Tribune Company would mark the start of a new era. Davis and many other young players would soon come of age under the Tribune regime.

of the championship Yankee teams he had played on. "They pick one another up, the way we used to," Berra explained. "If one guy stops hitting, somebody else starts." Chicago players, in turn, credited Durocher for sticking with them the year before and instilling a winning attitude. "In my early

days with the Cubs you wondered if you'd win," said Kessinger. "Now you go out there confident of victory." Santo stated it more simply: "With Leo on your side, you feel you can't lose."

Eventually, the '67 squad did start losing a bit more. The departure of left-handed hurler Ken Holtzman to the army and a second-half slump by outfielder Adolfo Phillips and other young players likely cost Chicago a pennant shot, but the Cubs still ended their revival year with a fine 87–74 record. The third-place finish was an almost unfathomable improvement over the previous year and was the best record by any Cubs squad since the 1945 NL champions.

Durocher had promised to give the Cubs "a winning habit," and he followed through on his word in just two years. Now his focus would be on completing the task. Over the next five years, as Leo sought his title, players and fans would enjoy the time of their lives.

Above: With the departure of Fergie Jenkins, Rick Reuschel emerged as the Cubs' best starting pitcher. The 6'3", 235-pound righty known as "Big Daddy" won in double figures each season from 1972 to 1980, peaking at 20–10 in '77. His older brother, Paul, joined him for four years, and on August 21, 1975, they combined on a shutout—a sibling big-league first. *Left:* Randy Hundley caught in a record 160 games in 1968 and squatted for 151 more during '69, when this photo was taken. The workload took its toll on the fine receiver, and knee injuries would limit the former Gold Glove winner to just 73 and 8 games in 1970 and '71.

LEO DUROCHER: MAN OF MANY WORDS

He earned his "Leo the Lip" nickname due to a propensity for arguing with umpires, but Leo Durocher had something to say no matter who was (or wasn't) listening. Here are a few quips from his 50-year baseball career:

- "Give me some scratching, diving, hungry ballplayers who come to kill you."
- "If I were playing third base and my mother were rounding third with the run that was going to beat us, I'd trip her. Oh, I'd pick her up and brush her off and say, 'Sorry, Mom,' but nobody beats me."
- "I never question the integrity of an umpire. Their eyesight, yes."
- "You don't save a pitcher for tomorrow. Tomorrow it might rain."

Ironically, Leo's most famous line—"Nice guys finish last"—was actually a misquote. While managing the Dodgers in the 1940s, he once said of the underachieving Giants, "Take a look at them. All nice guys. They'll finish last. Nice guys. Finish last." Sportswriters combined the last two sentences, and Durocher liked the new version so much he used it as the title of his autobiography.

The Cubs Reclaim Chicago

One look at Leo's face on this 1970 card and it was clear he still hadn't gotten over the '69 season. Few could blame him, but starting with an 11-game winning streak in April, his Cubs would contend for much of the 1970 campaign as well.

With the Cubs and American League White Sox both in pennant contention for most of the season, Chicago experienced baseball nirvana in the summer of '67. Close to one million fans took in the action on the South Side at Comiskey Park, while attendance at Wrigley Field leaped more than 50 percent to its highest point in a decade: 977,226.

The White Sox had outdrawn their struggling crosstown rivals for most of 15 years, and by nearly a 2-to-1 margin as recently as 1965, but by '67 the Cubs had almost completely erased this huge gap under Leo Durocher. They had even begun to dig into the White Sox fan base. In the years to come, as the Wrigley Field residents continued to contend while the South Siders fell into a tailspin, the pendulum would swing the other way.

Case in point: 1969. The 92–70 Cubs reached the zenith of their popularity in the Durocher era with a record 1,674,993 packing Wrigley to see their boys rise but dramatically fall. The White Sox, in contrast, were just 68–94, and the crowds at Comiskey fell off to 589,546. It got even worse in 1970: 1,642,705 for the Cubs, just 495,355 (or 6,115 per game) for the 56–106 "Dead Sox."

The ballparks and their surroundings also impacted the shift. Cavernous Comiskey was situated in a racially mixed part of Chicago impacted by the riots of the previous decade, and fears real and imagined kept many fans away. Wrigley, in contrast, was a cozier, fan-friendly locale in a neighborhood perceived to be much safer.

Later in the '70s, the American Leaguers would win back much of their legions with an improved club under new owner (and old Cubs executive) Bill Veeck. But they would never dominate the city's baseball affections as they had in the 1950–65 era. The Cubs were back to stay.

Just as he had 20 years earlier, Bill Veeck challenged for Chicago baseball supremacy in the mid-1970s. He assembled an ownership group and repurchased the White Sox. He and GM Roland Hemond constructed a team that contended in '77, but this time most Cubs fans did not defect.

The Bleacher Bums Set Up Residence

Starting in the late 1960s, a new group of fans could be spotted at Wrigley Field watching the rejuvenated Cubs do battle—and sometimes getting in on the battle themselves.

A group of about 75 construction workers—mostly beefy men clad in their yellow hard hats—began attending games before or after their shifts. Waiting in line to grab up some of the 23,000 unreserved tickets left available on game days, these "Bleacher Bums" would situate themselves in the left-field cheap seats and begin their task of heckling opposing outfielders into oblivion.

Occasionally they would get more physical; when the defending NL champion Cardinals came to town in August 1968, for instance, Lou Brock, Curt Flood, and Ron Davis had everything tossed at them from crumpled beer cups to flashlight batteries. As a way of fighting fire with fire, Flood put a sign on Brock's back reading "We're Still No. 1," which drew more boos and garbage. "I just got back from two weeks of army training, and that was safe compared with playing the outfield here if you don't wear a Cubs uniform," Davis said after one contest. "Come to think of it, I ought to get hazardous duty pay when I come here."

By 1969, with word of their exploits spreading to *The New York Times* and the Cubs in first place much of the summer, the "original" Bleacher Bums had been joined by high school and college kids wearing their own yellow helmets—hippies and hard hats, side by side. They'd cheer and sing throughout the game, and Chicago pitcher Dick Selma got into the act by waving a towel back at them from the bullpen. Selma didn't help the Cubs much as a hurler, but the Bums loved him. When he returned with the Phillies the next spring and donned a yellow helmet to lead them in pregame songs, they tossed him about $5 in coins as thanks.

"They were rabid and loud: They actually became our tenth man on the field," Cubs third baseman Ron Santo said of the '69 Bleacher Bums. "I truly believe they were a catalyst for success from Opening Day."

The Bleacher Bums enjoy another day of sunshine and baseball at Wrigley Field.

Billy Williams: Quiet Consistency

As a minor-leaguer, Billy Williams almost quit the game. As a major-leaguer, he played close to seven years without missing a game.

The Cubs had a lineup filled with All-Star-caliber ballplayers from 1967 to '73, but Williams was perhaps the most dependable and indispensable of them all. He possessed a smooth, powerful batting stroke that Chicagoans dubbed the "Sweet Swing." When it came to durability, nobody in baseball was better. A left-handed hitter who lacked the natural charisma of Banks or the feelings-on-his-sleeve intensity of fellow

Even when the team wasn't contending, one thing Cubs fans could always count on through the 1960s and early '70s was Billy Williams. He actually seemed to get better with age. In 1970, he topped the National League with 137 runs scored—the highest total in the circuit since Johnny Mize's 137 in 1947.

slugging mate Ron Santo, Williams simply went about his job for 1,117 consecutive games between 1963 and 1970, then an NL record.

Signed by the Cubs out of high school in 1956, Williams began progressing through the team's farm system. In the summer of '59, homesick and unsure of his abilities, he jumped the San Antonio club and headed home to tiny Whistler, Alabama. Chicago scout Buck O'Neil knew Billy and his parents, and he called on the family. He didn't pressure Williams about coming back but wisely suggested they go watch a game at the local ballpark. The young players there flocked to Billy (already a hometown hero), and within a few days he decided to return to San Antonio. O'Neil did the driving and ego-boosting.

The intervention proved effective. After two late-season trials in Chicago, Williams emerged as NL Rookie of the Year in 1961 with 25 home runs and 86 RBI—the first of 13 consecutive years the .290 career hitter would top the 20-homer, 80-RBI plateau in a pitching-dominated era. He never led the league in either power category, but his 392 homers and 1,353 RBI as a Cub rank third and fourth in franchise history.

Predominantly a left fielder (although he played right field in 1965 and 1966 and first base late in his career), Williams usually batted third in front of Santo and Banks while walking behind them in the spotlight. But fans and teammates knew full well his value, and the Sweet Swinger later joined Banks in both the Hall of Fame and the Cubs front office.

Billy Williams is still a favorite autograph to get at Wrigley Field.

Two seasons after losing MVP honors to Johnny Bench, Williams again finished second to Bench for MVP in 1972. This time the decision was more disputed. Williams almost won the Triple Crown with 37 homers, 122 RBI, and a league-leading .333 batting average that earned him the Silver Bat Award from NL President Charles Feeney.

BILLY THE IRON MAN

On September 22, 1963, Cubs left fielder Billy Williams returned from a day off to go 0-for-5 in a 7–3 win over the Braves at Wrigley Field. Exactly two months later, President John Kennedy was shot and killed in Dallas.

In the years to come, as the country endured tumultuous times, Williams continued showing up every day in the box scores. As he reached and passed the 500-game mark, U.S. troop levels and casualties in Vietnam mounted. And in the years just before he toppled Stan Musial's old National League record by playing in his 896th consecutive contest on June 29, 1969—Billy Williams Day at Wrigley—Robert Kennedy and Martin Luther King, Jr., were assassinated and racial riots broke out in Chicago and elsewhere. Through it all, Billy played on.

Finally, late in the 1970 season, manager Leo Durocher and Williams both decided the pressure of the streak was becoming a distraction. On September 3, Billy sat out a home contest against the Phillies and ended his string at 1,117 games. Steve Garvey would top his record in 1983, but Williams had already left a positive and permanent mark during a troubled time.

Even the ugly, ill-fitting Cubs road uniforms of the early 1970s couldn't hide the all-out style with which Santo played the game. Here he follows the path of his throw to first base, seemingly oblivious to the take-out slide attempted by Braves baserunner (and future Cubs manager) Dusty Baker.

Ron Santo: Cooperstown Credentials

Santo belted 342 career home runs, so it's appropriate for a fan to want his signature on a bat.

It is perhaps one of the more baffling of all decisions made by Hall of Fame voters and selection committees over the years, right up there with the failure to admit Buck O'Neil with other African American pioneers in 2006. Ron Santo—like O'Neil, a legend in Cubs annals—was one of the greatest offensive and defensive third basemen in history, yet for some 30 years he has remained an outsider looking in at the bronze plaques lining the walls of Cooperstown.

Certainly Santo's statistics merit consideration. The cleanup man in Chicago's lineup between Hall of Famers Billy Williams and Ernie Banks, the nine-time All-Star was good for 25 to 30 homers and 90 to

100 RBI every year in a period when few players reached either mark. He drove in at least 94 runs and finished in the NL's top ten in the category each year from 1963 to '70. All told, he had 1,290 RBI (fifth most in franchise history) and 337 homers (fourth best) as a Cub. Santo was a .277 career hitter who batted at or topped .300 on four occasions; he even led the league in triples during 1964 with 13 despite being slow afoot.

Santo shined defensively as well, pacing all NL third basemen in assists for seven straight seasons, putouts for six straight (and seven times overall), and double plays on six occasions en route to five Gold Glove Awards. Named team captain at age 25 in 1965, he was a more demonstrative player than the easygoing Banks and Williams, and he enjoyed having fiery Leo Durocher as manager until the two grew weary of each other after the team's '69 collapse. Had Chicago held on to its big NL East lead that season, Santo—who posted a career-high 123 RBI—may very well have been named National League MVP. He wound up fifth in the voting, one of his four appearances in the top eight.

Among the most popular players in franchise history despite his team's failure to reach the postseason, Santo has carved out a great second career of nearly 20 years as a Cubs broadcaster. The diabetes that he's battled since age 18 has ravaged his health, but he is still loved by Chicago fans who will always consider him one of the best—even if the Hall of Fame never calls.

SANTO'S SECRET

After Ron Santo homered off Bill Singer on September 25, 1968, he ran around the Wrigley Field bases faster than normal and then quickly headed for the clubhouse. Fans didn't know it, but Santo had been trembling and seeing double at the plate just before his blast, two signs that his blood sugar was dangerously low.

Santo is diabetic, a fact he kept secret from all but his teammates for most of his career. He was told he had the life-threatening disease the same day he signed with the Cubs; he learned to give himself insulin injections while playing through occasional cold sweats, double vision, and other bad reactions.

In July 1971, Santo decided to go public with his struggle, and he immediately became a role model and advocate for children and adults facing similar challenges. His Ron Santo Walk for the Cure has raised more than $55 million for diabetes research since its 1979 inception. Despite having both lower legs removed and countless other medical complications related to his disease, he's still in the radio booth calling games and rooting his Cubs on.

Left: Although wearing "traditional" home garb here, Santo actually donned the uniform of the crosstown rival White Sox at career's end. The near-miss Durocher Cubs were being broken up in the winter of 1973, and ownership granted his wish to stay in Chicago. After just one .221 season in Comiskey Park, however, he retired. *Above:* Santo signs an autograph for a volunteer at the 2006 Walk to Cure Diabetes.

ALL GAMES PLAYED PRIOR TO 1988 WERE DAY GAMES, WHICH MEANT THERE WAS PLENTY OF SUNSHINE FOR FANS TO CONTEND WITH AT WRIGLEY. THIS HAT HELPED BLOCK OUT THE RAYS.

Mr. Cub Cracks No. 500

CHICAGO, May 4, 1970—Ernie Banks joined baseball's top tier of sluggers when he hit his 500th home run today at Wrigley Field. Banks' blast, which came off a fastball from Atlanta's Pat Jarvis in the second inning, sailed over the wall behind Braves outfielder Henry Aaron. The milestone shot made Banks just the ninth player, including Aaron, to reach 500, and it also gave Banks 1,600 RBI in his career—a feat previously attained by just 11 big-leaguers.

As it was cold and miserable weather at Wrigley, only 5,264 fans saw Banks make history and Ron Santo win the 4–3 game with an 11th inning single.

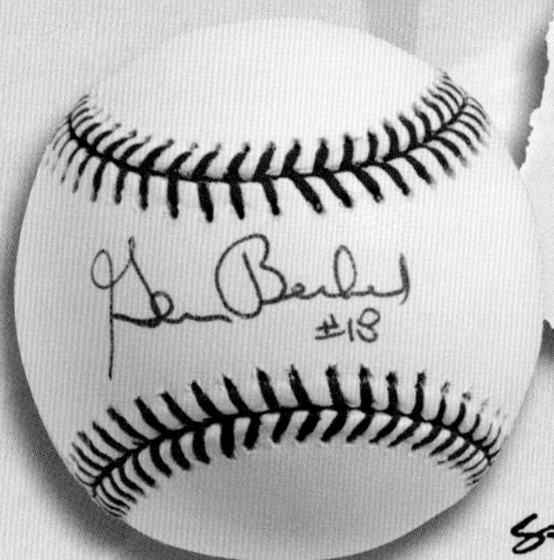

JUDGING FROM THE DATE PENCILED IN AT UPPER RIGHT, THE FAN WHO BOUGHT THIS PROGRAM SAW FERGIE JENKINS BEAT THE PHILLIES BEHIND TWO BILLY WILLIAMS HOMERS.

OFFICIAL PROGRAM 15¢

MAY 1 1971

7-4

CHICAGO CUBS · WRIGLEY FIELD

SECOND BASEMAN GLENN BECKERT WAS A CUBS MAINSTAY FROM 1965 TO '73, EARNING FOUR ALL-STAR SELECTIONS AND A GOLD GLOVE IN '68—WHEN HE ALSO HAD A 27-GAME HIT STREAK.

THIS MAN OF HONOR CELEBRATED HIS "DAY" BY BREAKING STAN MUSIAL'S NL RECORD FOR CONSECUTIVE GAMES PLAYED (895) AND COLLECTING FIVE HITS (INCLUDING TWO DOUBLES AND TWO TRIPLES) IN A DOUBLEHEADER.

BILL BUCKNER HAD 1,136 OF HIS 2,715 BIG-LEAGUE HITS AND 516 OF HIS 1,208 CAREER RBI WITH THE CUBS FROM 1977 TO '84.

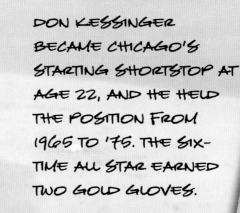

DON KESSINGER BECAME CHICAGO'S STARTING SHORTSTOP AT AGE 22, AND HE HELD THE POSITION FROM 1965 TO '75. THE SIX-TIME ALL STAR EARNED TWO GOLD GLOVES.

IN ADDITION TO "PITCHING" DONUTS ON THIS BUMPER STICKER, CHICAGO'S GREAT THIRD BASEMAN ENDORSED RON SANTO'S PIZZA—SOLD AT WRIGLEY FIELD AND SUBURBAN LOCALES.

THE SWEET SWING OF BILLY WILLIAMS PRODUCED NINE TOP 10 FINISHES IN THE NL HOME RUN RANKINGS—AND EIGHT ON THE RBI CHARTS—BETWEEN 1963 AND '72.

1969: The Glory and the Pain

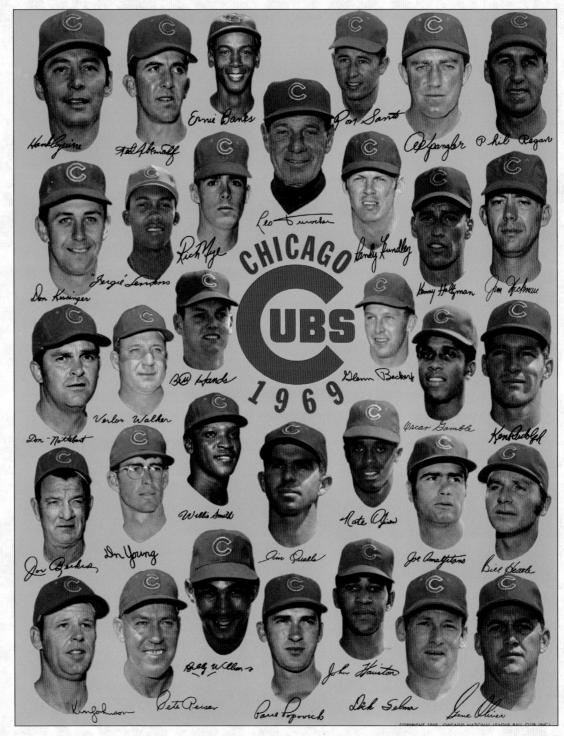

Nearly four decades later, it remains the one season Cubs fans will never forget. They recall with a glint in their eye the magical promise of spring and summer, then their voices lower to a hush when recounting September's dark downturn.

The year was 1969. Americans landed on the moon, rock enthusiasts flocked to Woodstock, and the Cubs seemed poised to finally return to the postseason. The most people to attend a home opener at Wrigley Field in 40 years—a standing-room crowd of 40,796—saw Chicago blow a 5–2, ninth-inning lead before prevailing 7–6 on a pinch-hit, two-run homer by utility outfielder Willie Smith in the 11th. Many of those deliriously cheering Smith's heroics sported buttons that read "Next Year Is This Year."

For a while the slogan seemed prophetic, as the tight-knit club began the season 11–1 and held first place every day into early September. Six hundred World Series ticket requests were being called in to Wrigley Field daily, and juke boxes and radio stations citywide blasted the team's unofficial theme song: "Hey, hey, holy mackerel, no doubt about it. The Cubs are on their way." The

The collapse of the '69 Cubs has been examined in many articles and books through the years. While Durocher is most often blamed for not resting his regulars, other points brought up include too many day games, a 14–16 record in doubleheaders (the Mets went 30–14), and the lack of a strong center fielder.

Here on-deck batter Ron Santo greets Henry Aaron after "Hammerin' Hank" scored on Willie McCovey's third-inning homer during the '69 All-Star Game. Had they not been overtaken by the Mets, Santo and his teammates would have played Aaron's Braves in the first NLCS that October.

North Siders placed five players on the NL All-Star squad—the entire infield plus catcher Randy Hundley. Ernie Banks found the fountain of youth at age 38, and captain Ron Santo took to clicking his heels after each victory to the delight of the Wrigley

faithful. When Fergie Jenkins shut out the Giants 3–0 on August 16, Chicago was 75–44 with a nine-game lead over the surprising New York Mets.

Then it all unraveled. The Cubs suddenly went cold, losing 11 of 12 in one stretch, and the red-hot Mets rapidly closed the gap. New York swept a two-game series with the leaders at Shea Stadium on September 8 and 9 to get within a half-game, then they shot into first with a doubleheader sweep of Montreal the next day. By the time the regular season concluded, the "Miracle Mets" were eight games in front of stunned Chicago. New York went 24–8 down the stretch, the Cubs 9–18.

What happened? Many pundits say manager Leo Durocher didn't rest his regulars enough during September, when every hitter in the lineup (with the exception of Billy Williams) seemed to slump simultaneously. Sure-handed fielders began making errors, and pitchers couldn't find the plate. "It was," said Durocher, "a total collapse."

Next year would have to wait—again.

HOLTZ'S NO-NOS

Other than his abbreviated perfect summer of '67, Ken Holtzman never reached the "next Sandy Koufax" status predicted for him in Chicago. There were two days, however, when baseball's "other" Jewish left-hander lived up to the hype.

On August 19, 1969, Holtzman pitched a 3–0 no-hitter against the Atlanta Braves before a crowd of 37,514 at Wrigley Field. Admitting

afterward that he lacked a decent curve and threw "98 to 100 percent fastballs" during the contest, he registered no strikeouts and survived several close calls—most notably a deep drive by Henry Aaron knocked down by the wind. Jubilant fans stormed the field after the victory, which earned "Holtzie" a $2,500 raise and kept the Cubs 7½ games ahead of the Mets in the NL East. Chicago's infamous September swoon, alas, would quickly reverse those standings.

A little less than two years later, on June 3, 1971, Holtzman registered his second no-hitter with a 1–0 victory at Cincinnati. He was just 25. Despite these flashes of brilliance, his overall Cubs record was a disappointing 80–81 by that year's end when he was traded.

Close but No Cigar:
The Cubs of the Early '70s

It would have been easy and understandable had the Cubs never recovered from the setback of 1969, but to their credit the same contingent of players remained a threat to win the National League East for the next several seasons. And while they could not recapture the hearts of the entire city as they had in '69—nothing ever compares to a first kiss— they continued to draw strong fan support.

The 1970 squad served quick notice that they were not shell-shocked from the previous fall by going on an 11-game winning streak in mid-April and holding first place well into June. They then streaked the other way with a 12-game losing skein, and although they couldn't regain the top spot, they stayed within two games of first place until the season's waning days. A reserve playing his last full season, Ernie Banks provided the year's top highlight with his 500th career home run.

In '71, the Cubs used a better-late-than-never philosophy to the pennant race. Stuck about ten games behind the Pittsburgh Pirates much of the year, they had crept to within $4^1/_2$ on August 23 when owner Philip Wrigley used the unconventional method of an open letter in Chicago's four daily newspapers to defend embattled manager Leo Durocher, whose authoritative, demanding style had begun to grate on many players. Wrigley's move exacerbated the tension, and the Cubs promptly lost 12 of 16 to ruin their chances.

Even Wrigley had turned on Durocher by 1972, as the Cubs made one last run at a division title with their old guard. Starting pitching was the strong suit, as five starters (led by Fergie Jenkins) won in double figures. The bullpen was suspect, however, and with only near-MVP Billy Williams cracking the 20-homer mark, Chicago lost 27 one-run games. Durocher resigned on July 25, before he could be fired, with the Cubs 46–44 and ten games back. Successor Whitey Lockman brought them home at a .600 clip (39–26), but the Pirates kept the same pace to win by 11. Chicago's second-place finish was the final straw for Wrigley, and the dismantling of a near-great club began.

Manny Sanguillen *(left)* and the Pirates were a nemesis for Cubs second baseman Glenn Beckert and his teammates from 1970 to '72, finishing first in the NL East each season while Chicago annually imploded. Beckert's surprising .342 average in '71 and his great defense helped the Cubs stay competitive.

Fergie Jenkins: From the Great White North to North Side Greatness

Although he won 115 games in the American League, Jenkins was appropriately enshrined at Cooperstown in 1991 as a Cub. His success while toiling in hitter-friendly Wrigley Field is reflected in the fact that since his 1973 trade, just three Cubs pitchers have won 20 games in a season for Chicago—and none more than once.

If Billy Williams was the most consistent everyday player on the Cubs during their revival, Fergie Jenkins was unquestionably the team's No. 1 pitcher—and a national hero in his native Canada.

Born in Chatham, Ontario (about 50 miles from Detroit), Ferguson Arthur Jenkins, Jr., was the son of a black, American-born mother and a father from Barbados who had played semi-professional baseball. Signed by the Phillies at age 19, the 6'5" right-hander's early pro years were rough. After facing terrible racial discrimination in the minor leagues, he languished in the bullpen when called up by Philadelphia in 1965.

Fergie's frustration ended when he was "stolen" in a trade on April 21, 1966, by the Cubs (along with Adolfo Phillips and John Herrnstein) for solid-but-declining pitchers Larry Jackson and Bob Buhl. Converted into a starter by new Chicago manager Leo Durocher that August, Jenkins quickly became one of the National League's best. Beginning in 1967, he went 20–13, 20–15, 21–15, 22–16, 24–13, and 20–12 through 1972. His ERA rose above 3.21 just once during this period, and he never compiled fewer than 289 innings or 20 complete games. In five of six years he recorded at least 236 strikeouts, and his impeccable control usually kept his total walks down around 60. Jenkins remains the only pitcher since 1960 to win 20 or more games in six straight seasons.

A solid fastball and a terrific slider were Fergie's top weapons, but he could also help himself with the bat. This was especially evident in his Cy Young season of '71, when he supplemented his 24 wins, 2.77 ERA, and 263 strikeouts with 6 home runs, 20 RBI, and a .478 slugging percentage. His offense kept him in the lineup late in close contests and helped him complete nearly half of his 594 career starts (including 30 of 39 that year alone).

A slide to 14–16 by Jenkins in 1973 prompted a trade to Texas, where he rebounded with a 25–12 season. By the time he finished his career back with the Cubs in 1983, he ranked among baseball's all-time leaders with 284 wins, 49 shutouts, and 3,192 strikeouts (against just 997 walks). A few years later, Jenkins became the first Canadian elected to the Baseball Hall of Fame.

Chicago's ace Jenkins routinely faced the top pitcher on opposing clubs, and for many years that was the Cardinals' Bob Gibson. The two had great battles, including Opening Day 1971 at Wrigley, when both pitched 10-inning complete games and Fergie won a three-hitter, 2–1, on a walk-off home run by Billy Williams.

CUBS RIGHTY MILT PAPPAS MADE PADRES HITTERS BLUE ON SEPTEMBER 2, 1972, PITCHING A NO-HITTER AT WRIGLEY IN WHICH HE MISSED A PERFECT GAME BY ONE PITCH.

Rookie Hooton hurls no-hitter as Cubs top Phillies, 4–0

CHICAGO, April 16, 1972—Continuing the mastery that has marked his brief big-league career, rookie Burt Hooton of the Cubs threw a 4–0 no-hitter against the Phillies today in just his fourth major-league start.

Hooton, a 21-year-old right-hander who went from the University of Texas to the Cubs last year, gave up seven walks but very few well-hit balls. In 30 innings since his June 1971 call-up, he has now allowed just eight hits. In one of those games, a September 15 contest with the Mets at Shea Stadium, he earned his first big-league win and tied a team record with 15 strikeouts.

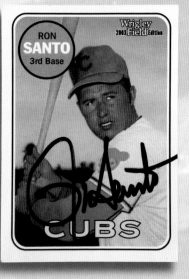

RON SANTO LOOKED DETERMINED TO MAKE THE CUBS WINNERS ON THIS REISSUE OF THE 1969 BASEBALL CARD. THE CLUB FELL SHORT, BUT HE HAD A CAREER-HIGH 123 RBI.

IRON MAN RANDY HUNDLEY HAD 18 HOMERS, 978 PUTOUTS, AND JUST EIGHT ERRORS IN 1969, HIS FOURTH STRAIGHT YEAR CATCHING 149 OR MORE GAMES.

BURT HOOTON SIGNED THIS BALL COMMEMORATING HIS NO-HITTER, WHICH WAS ACCOMPLISHED UNDER ROUGH CONDITIONS: 45 DEGREES, WITH A NORTH WIND OF 16 MILES-PER-HOUR WHIPPING THROUGH WRIGLEY FIELD.

IT'S A GOOD BET THAT MANY YOUNG CANADIANS FOUND ROOM AMID THE HOCKEY POSTERS ON THEIR WALLS FOR THIS ONE CELEBRATING THEIR COUNTRY'S GREATEST BASEBALL HERO.

VERY EARLY IN THEIR BASEBALL LIVES, MANY CHICAGOANS WERE INDOCTRINATED INTO THE ORDER OF CUBS FANDOM.

New Sports Posters from Sports Illustrated

WHEN CUBS FANS SAW NO. 31 WARMING UP IN THE BULLPEN BEFORE A GAME, THEY KNEW THEY WERE LIKELY TO SEE A WIRE-TO-WIRE PERFORMANCE BY THE STARTING PITCHER. BETWEEN 1967 AND '72, JENKINS COMPLETED 140 OF 234 STARTS—AND NEVER LESS THAN 20 IN ONE SEASON.

JENKINS
31

After Leo: Youth and Decline

Traded to the Cubs for Fergie Jenkins, Bill Madlock replaced Ron Santo at third base. He thrived despite the pressure, hitting .313, .354, and .339 from 1974 to '76 and winning batting titles the latter two years. His fiery personality, however, got him into trouble with management, and he was swapped to San Francisco for Bobby Murcer and others in 1977.

In six years under Leo Durocher, the Cubs finished second and third three times each and competed for a fistful of NL East pennants. Once an embattled Leo resigned late in the '72 season, however, the team took a rapid descent back into sub-.500 oblivion.

It wasn't all Durocher, of course. One by one, stalwarts from the contending teams of 1967–72 were traded away by general manager John Holland as the club undertook a massive youth movement. Pitcher Bill Hands was first to go after the 1972 campaign, and within two years he had been joined on the outbound train by his old batterymates Randy Hundley, fellow hurler Fergie Jenkins, and infield standouts Ron Santo, Glenn Beckert, Don Kessinger, and Billy Williams. As the familiar faces disappeared, promising rookies and second-year men replaced them, including Bill Madlock (for Santo at third), Andre Thornton (for Williams at first), and Burt Hooton and Rick Reuschel in the pitching rotation.

New manager Whitey Lockman let the kids undergo "on the job" training as the losses piled up. Fans, however, were not as patient. While the Cubs of Jenkins, Santo, and Williams had drawn more than 1.5 million fans each year from 1969 to '71, the '74 edition barely brought in one million customers. A managerial switch to Jim Marshall didn't help, and in 1976 Chicago celebrated 100 years in the National League with a second-straight 75–87 finish. Exciting players such as Dave Kingman, Bill Madlock, and Bill Buckner were brought aboard, but with the exception of Cy Young closer Bruce Sutter, little homegrown talent blossomed amid the ivy.

Interestingly, the Cubs did manage several surprising starts that suggested (falsely) brighter days lay ahead. Lockman had the '73 team in first place into late July before a horrible tailspin, and two years later Marshall's crew enjoyed life at the top for much of the first two months. Both teams finished under .500, as did every Chicago NL entrant through 1981 with the exception of the 81–81 crew of '77—which, naturally, started out 47–22 before the players remembered they were Cubs.

Acquired from the Dodgers before the 1977 season in a deal that also netted the Cubs shortstop Ivan DeJesus for Rick Monday, Bill Buckner delighted the Wrigley faithful with a .300 average, 235 doubles, and strong defense at first base over seven years. In 1980, he won the NL batting title with a .324 mark.

Sutter Saves, Wrigley Raves

In baseball, an ace relief pitcher is usually a requisite piece of a pennant-winning team. In the late 1970s, closer Bruce Sutter was often the key to whether the Cubs won at all.

From the moment he joined the team in May 1976, Sutter was a sensation. His devastating split-finger fastball—a pitch that resembled a regular heater until it plunged downward just as it crossed the plate—tied batters in knots and at times made the 6'2" right-hander virtually unhittable. Although the Cubs were never above .500 during his five years with the club, "Scooter" gave them a chance to win almost every time he took the mound.

Ironically, it was an elbow injury suffered in the low minors during 1973 that laid the groundwork for Sutter's success. The ensuing surgery robbed the 20-year-old of his strong fastball, but the next year he learned the split-finger version from roving pitching instructor Fred Martin and began using it in games. Within three years he was getting big-leaguers to lunge over it with frequency, and a Hall of Fame career was underway.

First used as a middle reliever with the Cubs, Sutter proved so effective as a rookie that by year's end he was the team's closer. Chicago wasn't expected to go anywhere in 1977, but thanks to their new phenom they contended much of the summer. Despite a midseason spell on the disabled list, Sutter finished with 31 saves, a 1.35 ERA, and 129 strikeouts in just 107 innings. Fans at Wrigley took to chanting "Scooter! Scooter!" in the late innings of close games, and he rewarded their faith by notching 27 more saves in 1978 and a league-leading 37 in '79—when he had a 2.23 ERA and earned the National League Cy Young Award.

Such accomplishments earned Sutter a $700,000 contract in an arbitration hearing after the 1979 season, but the Wrigley family refused to give him another big deal and traded him to the Cardinals for Leon Durham, Ken Reitz, and Tye Waller in December 1980. He later helped St. Louis win the '82 World Series title and eventually notched 167 of his 300 career saves with the Cards and Braves. But to the Bleacher Bums, he'll always be a Cub.

Bruce Sutter is pictured pitching a game in 1978, when he had 27 saves. That year, he gave up only 34 walks and had 106 strikeouts over 99 innings.

THE RAUCOUS NEW CUBS
Ron Santo leads off first

ERNIE BANKS SLUGGED 512 HOME RUNS FROM 1953 TO '71 AND TIED FOR SIXTH ALL TIME WITH EDDIE MATHEWS. HIS NO. 14 WAS THE FIRST NUMBER RETIRED BY THE CUBS.

WHEN THIS MAGAZINE HIT NEWSSTANDS ON MONDAY MORNING, JUNE 30, 1969, THE CUBS LED THE METS BY 7½ GAMES. THUS JINXED, CHICAGO PROMPTLY LOST SEVEN OF TEN GAMES.

Monday's act of patriotism overshadows Dodgers victory

LOS ANGELES, April 25, 1976—The Dodgers beat the Cubs 5–4 today at Chavez Ravine, but all anybody could talk about afterward was the great "save" made by Chicago center fielder Rick Monday.

In the bottom of the fourth inning, a man and boy suddenly jumped out of the stands and laid out an American flag in left-center. As they readied to set it on fire, Monday sprinted over and snatched it from their hands. He received a huge ovation as police took away the perpetrators. "If you're going to burn the flag, don't do it in front of me," said Monday. "I've been to too many veterans' hospitals and seen too many broken bodies of guys trying to protect it."

RESIDENTS BEYOND WRIGLEY'S OUTFIELD FENCES WHO FOUND BALLS ON THEIR ROOFTOPS IN 1978–80 DIDN'T NEED DAVE KINGMAN'S SIGNATURE TO KNOW WHO LIKELY HIT THEM THERE.

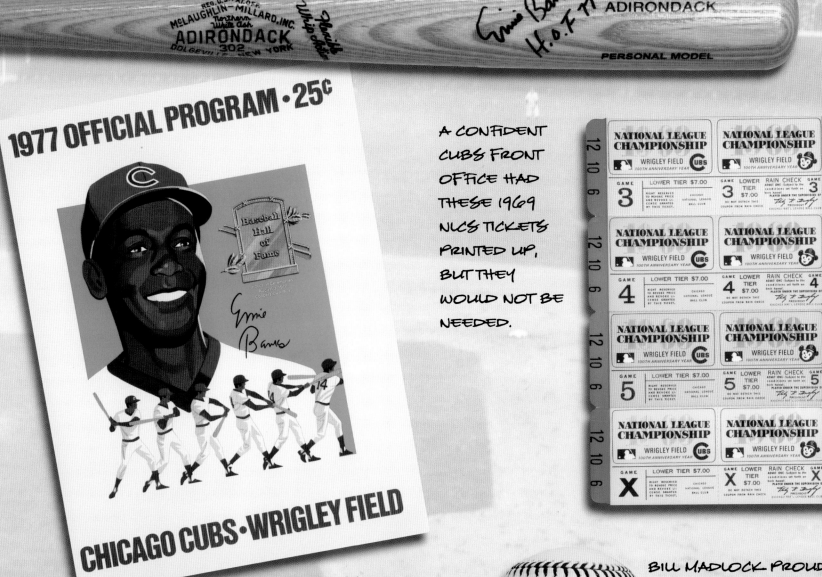

1977 OFFICIAL PROGRAM · 25¢

CHICAGO CUBS · WRIGLEY FIELD

A CONFIDENT CUBS FRONT OFFICE HAD THESE 1969 NLCS TICKETS PRINTED UP, BUT THEY WOULD NOT BE NEEDED.

AS THE '77 TEAM WILTED IN AUGUST, FANS PURCHASING THIS PROGRAM SALUTING "MR. CUB'S" HALL OF FAME INDUCTION LIKELY PINED FOR HIS PRESENCE IN THE LINEUP.

BILL MADLOCK PROUDLY MARKED BALLS HE AUTOGRAPHED WITH THE YEARS OF HIS FOUR NL BATTING TITLES, THE FIRST TWO OF WHICH HE EARNED WITH THE CUBS.

P. K. Wrigley's Legacy

Philip Wrigley tosses a ball in the air after a meeting with Cubs officials on January 9, 1964. To his left is rookie catcher Dick Bertell.

After originally saying he never wanted the job, Philip "P. K." Wrigley served as president of the Chicago Cubs for quite a long time: 43 years, to be exact. Inheriting ownership of the team from his father in 1932, he had reluctantly assumed the presidency two years later and kept the franchise and its ballpark in the city's hearts through many ups and downs—including long periods of on-field and fiscal losses—until his death at age 82 on April 12, 1977.

Wrigley was often criticized in some circles for his lack of baseball knowledge, and at the time of his death had reportedly not even seen a game in years at the North Side ballpark named for his father. But even if some of his innovations, such as the ill-fated "College of Coaches," bordered on the ridiculous, there is no denying that the single *best* move Wrigley made in the latter stage of his tenure was hiring Leo Durocher to manage the Cubs before the 1966 season. Although the egotistic, bombastic Durocher was a sharp contrast to the quiet, celebrity-shunning owner, the pair worked well alongside general manager John Holland in assembling a Cubs team that competed annually for league and division titles from 1967 to '72.

The changing landscape of the game, however, seemed to trouble Wrigley. He once said that he didn't believe any ballplayer was worth $100,000 a season and often arranged to trade Cubs players whose contracts were up for renewal. The one thing P. K. never cut corners on was Wrigley Field. He kept the ballpark looking new throughout his tenure, which was part of a philosophy focused on customer satisfaction. Unlike the team, the old place never let him down.

With Wrigley's death, ownership of the Cubs passed down to his only son, William. The elder Wrigley was grooming his boy to take over his entire business empire, not just the baseball club. With this in mind, William appointed another man—William Hagenah, Jr.—as team president. The first family of chewing gum still held the controls, but now they would no longer be in the spotlight.

A Day at the Ballpark, 1975

By the mid-1970s, Wrigley Field had become a kid- and family-dominated park. Serious baseball fans were largely staying away because the Cubs had sunk again in the standings after the heady years of Leo Durocher. Those old-timers who did come out, however, appreciated the fact that the cozy confines looked much the same as they had for generations. It was a deep contrast to the huge, concrete "cookie cutter" stadiums that were then popping up throughout the country.

A day at the corner of Clark and Addison was still an affordable endeavor for most folks. Box seats, though not often filled, cost $4.50, and reserved grandstands $3.50. Lower and upper deck grandstand seats were $2.50 for adults and $1.25 for kids, making a trip to Wrigley Field an excellent value for parents hoping to get their little ones a glimpse of Bill Madlock or Rick Monday. The Bleacher Bums had made sitting in the outfield seats fashionable again, and it cost just $1.25 to bake oneself in the Wrigley sun. Scorecards remained a quarter, with pencils a dime extra.

As always, fans could easily get to the park by public transportation. A train line let folks out just a block away, and two different bus routes went straight to Wrigley. There was plenty of parking available for those driving in from the suburbs; the Wrigleyville neighborhood had yet to undergo its 1980s resurgence. Night games, of course, were nonexistent.

Wrigley's menu had not changed much over the years. Fans could still get their fill of hot dogs, smoky links, peanuts, popcorn, and Cracker Jack, and there was beer, soda, and ice cream with which to cool off. If spectators wanted a head start on refreshments, they could stop by any of the bars outside the park—including Ernie's Bleachers, a drive-up hot dog stand that sold beer by the pail. And if they couldn't get to the game, they could learn the outcome with a glance at the two lights atop the center-field flagpole: green for a victory, red for a loss.

The bleachers are packed with fans on a sunny day at beautiful Wrigley Field.

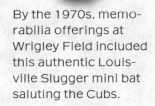

By the 1970s, memorabilia offerings at Wrigley Field included this authentic Louisville Slugger mini bat saluting the Cubs.

CHAPTER SEVEN

THE TRIBUNE ERA: 1982-PRESENT

WITH NEW OWNERSHIP, a renewed focus, and new lights, the Cubs returned to the postseason—but not with enough consistency. Great players including Sandberg, Dawson, Sosa, and Wood emerged, and broadcaster Harry Caray and Wrigley Field itself became the faces of Cubs baseball to a nationwide audience. And in 2007, a worst-to-first transformation provided hope for the future.

Left: The tradition of fans singing "Take Me Out to the Ballgame" during the seventh-inning stretch originated at White Sox games during the 1970s. Owner Bill Veeck heard legendary broadcaster Harry Caray singing in his booth and suggested he ask others to join in. Here Harry—with the Cubs—leads a Wrigley rendition in 1989 as his TV partner Steve Stone looks on. *Right:* Sammy Sosa provided summer-long headlines in 1998, but it was a team accomplishment that took center stage at season's end. The Cubs defeated the San Francisco Giants 5–3 in a one-game playoff at Wrigley Field on September 28, earning their first playoff appearance in nine years as the National League wild card entry.

Tribune Buys Team, Dallas in Chicago

For 65 years, through good times and bad, pennants and last-place finishes, one thing had remained constant for the Chicago Cubs: Wrigley family ownership. On June 16, 1981, four years after the death of P. K. Wrigley, that era ended when his son William—the third generation of the clan to own the club—sold it for $20.5 million to the Tribune Company.

A privately owned broadcasting conglomerate, the company's media holdings included both the *Chicago Tribune* daily newspaper as well as both WGN-TV and WGN Radio, which had been airing Cubs games since these stations first went on the air. The Tribune Company had formed its superstation WGN cable satellite station the same year, and one of its first moves upon buying the team was to make Cubs games available to a nationwide cable audience. That decision made uproarious play-by-play announcer Harry Caray a household name, and it introduced millions of Americans (and potential fans) to the beauty of Wrigley Field.

Whereas the team presidents employed by Bill Wrigley after his father's death were businessmen with limited or no baseball experience, the Tribune Company made an important step in turning around the fortunes of a team that had not finished in first place since 1945 by hiring "baseball lifer" Dallas Green as executive vice-president and general manager on October 15, 1981. An intense, physically imposing man at 6'5", the 47-year-old Green had been with the Philadelphia Phillies since the 1960s, first as a journeyman pitcher, then as the franchise's farm director, and most recently as manager of its first-ever World Series winner in 1980.

Green had been largely responsible for transforming the Phillies from one of baseball's worst franchises to a perennial

When Chicago defeated the Braves 5–1 in Atlanta on October 5, 2003, to clinch their NL Division Series, fans flooded into the streets around dormant Wrigley Field to celebrate the Cubs' first postseason series win of any kind since 1908.

Gary Gaetti, picked up by the Cubs for the 1998 stretch drive on his 40th birthday, hit .320 in 37 games and was a big factor in the winner-take-all wild card playoff. His two-run homer in the fifth gave Chicago a 2–0 lead, which they extended to 5–0 before a San Francisco rally in the ninth fell short.

playoff team. Now, just four days after his club's most recent postseason concluded, he resigned and accepted an offer from new Cubs chairman Andrew McKenna to help head up his old NL East rival. His five-year contract was worth $1 million, very lucrative for the time.

Never one to hide his feelings, the confident Green spoke of "building a new tradition" at Wrigley Field. "The Cubs have not been successful, and somebody has to take responsibility for that," he said. "I'm going to look everybody in the eye and tell them if they don't want to work as hard as I do, they might as well go home right now." In the days to come he further ruffled feathers by insisting that the Cubs install lights at the ballpark to compete in the modern baseball marketplace for free-agent players.

Tackling the more immediate concerns of a last-place club, he brought in his old Philadelphia coach (and former Cub utilityman) Lee Elia as manager, then pulled off a whopper of an all-shortstop trade: Ivan DeJesus to the Phillies for Larry Bowa and Ryne Sandberg. The veteran Bowa would start for three seasons in Chicago, while Sandberg would become one of the greatest second basemen in history.

Other key deals made in Green's busy first three years netted Cubs outfielders Keith Moreland, Bob Dernier, and Gary Matthews, as well as pitchers Steve Trout, Dick Ruthven, Dennis Eckersley, Scott Sanderson, and Rick Sutcliffe. When Elia lashed out at Wrigley fans during an early season tirade in 1983, Green won points in Wrigleyville by firing his old friend and naming Jim Frey manager. Ron Cey was acquired from the Dodgers, and with this nucleus in place (plus some homegrown talent), Chicago came within one game of reaching the 1984 World Series. The GM deservedly got much of the credit, and one fan recommended to the *Tribune* that the Cubs honor their boss by calling themselves the "Big Green Machine."

The years to come would not be as successful, and Green resigned under pressure after the 1987 season. But for helping return playoff baseball to Wrigley, his place in team history was assured.

Steve Trout, who spent five seasons with each Chicago team, had a career year in 1984 to help the Cubs to the NL East title. The lefty compiled a 13–7 record with a 3.41 ERA, and then added a 4–2 win against San Diego in the NLCS.

Sam Sianis, Billy's nephew, is the current owner of the Billy Goat Tavern.

THE BILLY GOAT CURSE

One would think a team could not be any more cursed after appearing in six-consecutive World Series without winning one, but in making it seven postseason setbacks, the 1945 Cubs dug themselves a deeper hole—thanks to one angry fan and one smelly goat.

Among those stepping up to the turnstiles at Wrigley Field for Game 4 of the '45 World Series was Billy Sianis, proprietor of a downtown Chicago restaurant known as the Billy Goat Tavern. Sianis had two tickets, one for himself and one for his goat, Sonovia. The goat was denied admission because, his owner was informed, "He smells." An irate Sianis put a hex on the Cubs, stating that they would never play in another World Series. They lost Game 4, lost the series in seven, and have indeed not returned since. Sianis apparently took the curse off a year before his 1970 death, but it has taken on renewed life in recent years as the Cubs have had some epic postseason meltdowns in stretching their fall classic famine to 63 years. BAAAAAAAD luck indeed.

Holy Cow! Harry Caray, WGN Emerge as Stars

Even before the Cubs became winners again in 1984, they were already providing quality entertainment to fans throughout Chicago and the country thanks to cable superstation WGN and its insightful, hilarious broadcaster Harry Caray.

Caray was no stranger to Chicagoans, having been the TV and radio voice of the White Sox for 11 years before the Tribune Company enticed him to switch leagues and replace retiring legend Jack Brickhouse in 1982. Harry's baseball roots also included a 1945–69 radio stint with the St. Louis Cardinals and powerful KMOX, which had delivered his outspoken, outrageous play-by-play across the Midwest. Still, he likely never expected the celebrity he'd achieve due to cable TV. The new medium caught on nationwide just as Caray was catching on with the Cubs. Suddenly people everywhere were spending their afternoons with the ageless, funny-looking guy with the big glasses who loved to shout "Holy Cow!" after big plays and "Cubs Win! Cubs Win!" when they did—which most years wasn't often. Caray often butchered players' names, but viewers didn't seem to mind.

The Harry phenomenon took hold quickly. WGN reached eight million cable households nationwide in 1981 and 20 million just five years later. Fans and autograph seekers descended on Caray, and his ritual of leaning out of his booth during the seventh-inning stretch and singing "Take Me Out to the Ballgame" with the Wrigley crowd—always wonderfully off-key—became as much a tradition as the ballpark's outfield ivy. His enthusiasm, sincere love for the game, and baseball knowledge all came through in his broadcasts, which endeared him to everybody from seasoned North Side fans to the Boston housewife looking to pass a few hours before dinner. When Caray returned to work after a 1987 stroke, President Ronald Reagan, himself a former Cubs broadcaster, called midgame to welcome him back. Harry chatted for a bit, said goodbye, then quickly told viewers how "Rob" Dernier had reached first. (He goes by Bob.)

Named the winner of the Ford Frick Award by the Baseball Hall of Fame in 1989, Caray got the thrill of his life two years later when he covered a Cubs-Braves game with his son Skip and grandson Chip, both then Atlanta announcers. And two months after Caray's February 1998 death at 83, Dutchie, his widow, came to Wrigley and sang "Take Me Out to the Ballgame" alongside Chip, his grandpa's successor.

There was only one Harry Caray, but his famous face is such a joy for Cubs fans to behold that many of them like trying it on themselves. Harry masks like this one are available at his popular Chicago restaurants, and one man even donned Harry glasses and a wig to rob a bank.

Harry Caray died in 1998 after 16 years as the beloved "voice" of the Cubs, and the next year the team erected this statue at Wrigley Field in his memory. It depicts Caray and his Wrigley fans at the moment in each game both loved best—their sing-along during the seventh-inning stretch.

1984: End of the 39-Year Drought

In between his days as a cocky young fire-baller and a lights-out closer, Dennis Eckersley was an effective member of Chicago's starting rotation. Acquired from Boston for Bill Buckner in early 1984, he went 10–8 with a 3.03 ERA to help the Cubs reach the postseason and then followed it up with an 11–7 slate in '85.

Baby boomers born the year the Cubs last reached the World Series had already celebrated their 20th high school reunions by the time new manager Jim Frey gathered his troops at spring training in 1984 to begin their latest postseason quest. When the Cubs completed their exhibition schedule at 7–20—the worst mark in baseball—it looked like another sixth place finish was in store.

To their credit, 33,436 faithful showed up at Wrigley for the home opener. They were rewarded with an 11–2 thrashing of the Mets. As the weeks passed, those observing the Cubs noticed a new confidence taking hold. Young players such as catcher Jody Davis, first baseman Leon Durham, and second baseman Ryne Sandberg were developing well. Veterans brought in by GM Dallas Green, including Gary Matthews, Bob Dernier, and Ron Cey, were providing experience and strong play. For the first time in six years, the Cubs entered June with a winning record.

Green, however, had bigger goals in mind than a .500 season. On June 13 he pulled off a huge deal, trading four talented youngsters (Joe Carter, Mel Hall, Don Schulze, and Darryl Banks) to the Indians for more veteran support (catcher Ron Hassey and pitchers Rick Sutcliffe and George Frazier). The move was Green's statement that he believed the team could contend *now*. When Sutcliffe stepped into the rotation and immediately became the league's hottest pitcher, the deal won public support. The bearded right-hander went 16–1 in just over three months. With the slick-fielding Sandberg emerging as an offensive force and MVP candidate, the Cubs had two players capable of carrying them to October.

They got there, too, winning the NL East title with help from many other sources: steady starting pitchers Dennis Eckersley, Steve Trout, and Scott Sanderson; ace reliever Lee Smith; balanced production (six players with 80 or more RBI); and the clubhouse leadership of Matthews. More than two million fans (2,107,655) packed Wrigley to see the show, an attendance figure that shattered the club's previous high-water mark of 1,674,993 set in the fateful summer of 1969. Harry Caray spread the gospel to millions more nationwide over superstation WGN. The Cubs became the feel-good story of the baseball year—and were ready to finally write another chapter in their rich postseason history.

Leon Durham came to the Cubs in December 1980 as part of the big Bruce Sutter trade, and he quickly matured into a first-rate player. Initially an outfielder, he took over at first base after Bill Buckner's departure in early '84 and hit .279 with 23 homers and 96 RBI that division-winning summer.

Super at Second: Ryne Sandberg

Although Dante Bichette of the Rockies was safe on this play, "Ryno" almost always made the key defensive play when needed. He won nine consecutive Gold Gloves at second base between 1983 and 1991, one less than Roberto Alomar's major-league record for the position.

Few players ever got off to a more inauspicious start with the Cubs than Ryne Sandberg. Few in major-league history ever became as terrific an all-around performer.

Sandberg was considered by fans to be the "throw-in" piece of the all-shortstop deal on January 27, 1982, which sent Ivan DeJesus to the Phillies in exchange for Ryne and All-Star Larry Bowa.

His unique first name had been picked out by his expectant parents after watching Yankee reliever Ryne Duren pitch. Highly recruited as a high school quarterback in Spokane, Washington, Sandberg was set to play at Washington State until the Phillies drafted him in 1978. Called up late in '81, the skinny shortstop's only hit in six at-bats for Philadelphia came at Wrigley Field on September 27; little did Cub fans know they were looking at their own team's next superstar player.

Here is where fate intervened. Dallas Green, manager of the Phillies, was hired away to be the Cubs' general manager after the 1981 season. He saw Sandberg's potential,

Left: Sandberg usually rose to the occasion offensively, so it was no surprise when he "celebrated" his retirement announcement on August 2, 1997 (effective season's end) with two homers against the Dodgers. Earlier that year, he had passed Joe Morgan as the new home run king among second basemen with his 267th at the position. *Right:* When fans in the crowd yelled out "We love you, Ryne!" during Sandberg's 2005 Hall of Fame induction speech, Cooperstown's newest member waved and called back "I love you, too." His address focused on the respect he had for the game, because "the name on the front [of the uniform] is a lot more important than the one on the back."

"THE SANDBERG GAME"

Ryne Sandberg had already proven himself a top-notch fielder and offensive spark plug early in the 1984 season. That June 23, however, the fans at Wrigley Field and a nationwide TV audience watching the NBC Game of the Week saw the unveiling of a superstar.

The Cubs were trailing St. Louis 9–8 in the bottom of the ninth with old pal Bruce Sutter on the mound for the Cardinals. Sutter was having so dominant a season that broadcaster Bob Costas assumed the contest was over, and he began naming Willie McGee NBC's "Player of the Game." He forgot to tell Sandberg, however, who homered off Sutter to tie the score. St. Louis went ahead again in the tenth, but once more Sandberg smashed a Sutter pitch out of the park, paving the way for the Cubs to win 12–11 an inning later on Dave Owen's pinch-single.

All told, Sandberg was 5-for-6 with seven RBI on a day Cubs fans still refer to simply as "The Sandberg Game." Certainly Cardinals manager Whitey Herzog wouldn't forget it. Afterward, he called Chicago's second baseman "the greatest player I've ever seen."

and playing it cool, he managed to get the Phils to include him in the teams' shortstop swap that winter. Installed at third base (Chicago put Bowa at short), Ryne got off to a 1-for-32 start. Manager Lee Elia stuck with him, however, and Sandberg finished the year with a .271 average and 32 steals.

Moved to second base in 1983, Sandberg hit just .261 but won the first of nine straight Gold Gloves. The next summer was a magical one for both him and the Cubs, as the team won its first-ever NL East title and "Ryno" turned in an MVP season: 200 hits, 36 doubles, 19 triples, 19 homers, 84 RBI, 32 steals, a .314 average, and stellar defense.

He emerged as the classic five-tool player and became a favorite of fans, teammates, and opponents.

For most of the next 15 years, the future Hall of Famer was the king of Wrigley Field, hitting as many as 40 home runs, stealing as many as 54 bases, and setting defensive records with 123 consecutive errorless games at second and four seasons without a throwing error. Blessed with great range, great instincts, and virtually no ego, the 10-time All-Star retired with 403 doubles, 344 steals, and 1,318 runs scored—including a then-record 277 homers as a second baseman. Not bad for a throw-in.

Balls like this one made a nice keepsake for Cubs fans making the trip to Cooperstown for Sandberg's 2005 induction.

1989 NATIONAL LEAGUE

CHICAGO CUBS

EASTERN DIVISION CHAMPIONS

THE "BOYS OF ZIMMER"— WHO IN '89 WENT A SURPRISING 93-69 UNDER THE NL'S MANAGER OF THE YEAR—WERE SALUTED ON THIS PENNANT SOLD AT WRIGLEY.

CLOSER LEE SMITH, WHO REGULARLY BLAZED BALLS BY HITTERS DURING HIS CUB TENURE, TOOK TIME TO MARK THIS ONE WITH HIS LOFTY LIFETIME SAVE TOTAL.

IN 1998, THE CUBS HONORED THE MEMORY OF BELOVED BROADCASTER HARRY CARAY BY WEARING THIS PATCH BEARING HIS LIKENESS ON THEIR UNIFORM SLEEVES.

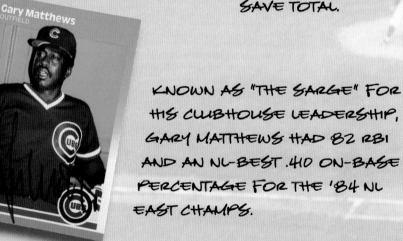

Gary Matthews
OUTFIELD

FLEER

Four-run seventh propels Padres past Cubs, into World Series

SAN DIEGO, Oct. 7, 1984—The Padres clinched their first World Series berth in franchise history and completed a stirring NLCS comeback today with a 6–3 victory at Jack Murphy Stadium over the sputtering Cubs.

Down 3–0 to Chicago ace Rick Sutcliffe after two innings, San Diego scored twice in the sixth and four times in the seventh as four relievers held the Cubs scoreless the rest of the way. Big hits during the game-breaking rally included a two-run double by Tony Gwynn and a follow-up single by series MVP Steve Garvey. It marked the third straight loss in the best-of-five series by the Cubs, who won the first two games at Wrigley Field and needed just one more to clinch.

KNOWN AS "THE SARGE" FOR HIS CLUBHOUSE LEADERSHIP, GARY MATTHEWS HAD 82 RBI AND AN NL-BEST .410 ON-BASE PERCENTAGE FOR THE '84 NL EAST CHAMPS.

THIS NLCS SCORECARD AND TICKET STUB PROVIDED A NICE KEEPSAKE FOR A CUB FAN, ESPECIALLY WITH ANDRE DAWSON'S SIGNATURE ADORNING THE COVER. THE CUBS, ALAS, LOST THE SERIES.

THROUGH WINNING SEASONS AND LEAN YEARS, FIRST BASEMAN MARK GRACE REMAINED A STEADY, CLASSY STAR FOR THE CUBS FROM 1988 TO 2000. IN THE '89 NLCS, HE HIT .647.

THE RIVALRY BETWEEN CHICAGO'S TWO BIG-LEAGUE TEAMS WAS CAPTURED ON THIS BEER MUG ADORNED WITH THE CARTOON LIKENESSES OF CUBS MANAGER JIM FREY AND WHITE SOX SKIPPER TONY LARUSSA.

SECOND IN MOST VALUABLE PLAYER VOTING TWICE WITH THE EXPOS, ANDRE DAWSON FINALLY EARNED THE HONOR IN 1987 WITH THE CUBS. COOPERSTOWN MAY BE NEXT.

The Big Letdown

Cubs fans hoped that the wild ride of '84 would mark the start of a new era of dominance. It turned out instead to be a one-year diversion in a dreadful stretch of losing.

The tight, well-rounded club that had stormed to a divisional title the previous year was decimated by injuries in 1985. Starting pitchers Rick Sutcliffe, Steve Trout, Dennis Eckersley, and Scott Sanderson all missed considerable action, as did outfielders Gary Matthews and Bob Dernier. Only Eckersley won as many as ten games, and offensive production fell off from six 80-RBI men to just two: Keith Moreland and Ryne Sandberg. Cruising along in first place in mid-June, Chicago suddenly hit the skids with a club record-tying 13-game losing streak from which it never recovered. By year's end, the Cubs were in fourth with a 77–84 record—a 19-win drop-off in just one season.

Things didn't improve in '86. The club got off to a terrible start that cost manager Jim Frey his job, and new skipper Gene Michael had no answers either as the plight of the once-solid pitching staff continued. Sutcliffe, destiny's darling just two years before, was 5–14; Eckersley 6–11; Sanderson 9–11. The team ERA of 4.49 was the league's worst, and on offense even Sandberg had an off year. A woeful Pirates squad saved the Cubs from the indignity of last place, but the Cubs' 70–90 record left them 37 games behind the Mets in the NL East—their worst end-of-year deficit in a quarter century.

In 1987, the three-year journey from first to worst was completed as Chicago fell to sixth. There were some bright spots: Andre Dawson turned in an MVP performance during his first year with the club, and Sutcliffe rebounded to lead the league in wins. Rick had little help in the rotation, however, as the team ERA ballooned even more to 4.55 and negated a much-improved offense that led the National League with 209 homers—most in the NL since 1956. Dawson cranked out 49 longballs, while Moreland and Leon Durham contributed 27 each. Fans liked the action, as Chicago became the first last-place club in league history to draw two million fans. But it sure wasn't '84.

Top: A common scene during the dismal summer of '85 was manager Jim Frey *(center)* going to the mound as yet another pitcher struggled. Here George Frazier and catcher Steve Lake chat with Frey at Dodger Stadium. *Right:* A bright spot during the losing 1985–87 seasons was the continued dominance of closer Lee Smith. The 6'6", 225-pound right-hander had 33, 31, and 36 saves during this period. Upon departing for Boston in a dreadful trade for journeyman pitchers Calvin Schiraldi and Al Nipper in 1988, Smith had a team-record 180 saves—with 298 more to come in his Cooperstown-worthy career.

Fill in the Blank:
Dawson Proves a Bargain

oping to squelch the rising salary demands of ballplayers, major-league owners quietly agreed in the winter of 1987 not to sign each other's free agents. In the case of outfielder Andre Dawson, however, Cubs general manager Dallas Green got an offer he just couldn't refuse.

Rookie of the Year while with the Expos in 1977 and MVP runner-up four years later, Dawson had been one of baseball's best all-around players—hitting for power and average while providing speed on the bases and stellar defense in right field. His problem was the hard artificial surface at Montreal's Olympic Stadium, which wreaked havoc on his knees and his numbers. By the '86 season, while still only 32, "The Hawk" was limited to just 130 games and was no longer considered a 30-homer, 30-steal threat.

A free agent that winter, Dawson was convinced that he could jump-start his career if given the opportunity to play every day in an outfield with real (and thus softer)

grass. Setting his sights on the Cubs, Dawson and his agent Dick Moss made overtures during spring training that went largely ignored due to the owners' agreement. Finally, in desperation, Dawson and Moss hatched a novel plan. They gave Green a blank contract and their word that the six-time Gold Glove winner would sign for whatever figure the GM felt was justified. Green finally relented, and on March 6, Dawson signed a one-year, $500,000 deal that made him just the 15th-highest paid Cub.

Dawson would earn every penny, plus $200,000 in incentive bonuses. Playing in 153 games in 1987, he led the NL with 49 homers, 137 RBI, and 353 total bases (all career highs). He hit for the cycle in April, earned a seventh Gold Glove in right, and became the first player on a last-place team to win the National League MVP Award. Hugely popular with teammates and the Wrigley fans, who would bow to him from the outfield bleachers after big plays, he wound up hitting 174 of his 438 career homers as a Cub. And by the time he left town as a free agent five years later, The Hawk was making $3.3 million a year.

After his MVP year in 1987, Dawson continued to be a productive power threat for five more years in Chicago. "The Hawk" averaged 26 homers and 90 RBI from 1988 to '92, and in the field he earned his eighth and final Gold Glove in '88.

With due respect to Ernie Banks, it's hard to imagine a player who could appreciate Wrigley Field more than Andre Dawson. The soft grass soothed his knees and allowed him to reclaim his status as a top-flight defensive and offensive player.

Let There Be Light(s)

Having experienced many dark days in their recent history, the Cubs brightened things up in 1988 with the installation of lights at Wrigley Field.

Ever since 1935, when night ball debuted in the major leagues at Cincinnati's Crosley Field, Cubs management, fans, and sportswriters had pondered the topic. Team owner Philip "P. K." Wrigley had actually readied to fit his own ballpark with lights after the 1941 season, but Pearl Harbor intervened and Wrigley donated the unused equipment to the war effort. Once the war ended, more teams intrigued by the higher attendance at night games joined the trend. By 1948, every big-league park but Wrigley Field was playing after dark.

Asked his reasoning for standing firm, P. K. offered various excuses, including chivalry: "In deference to people living around our ballpark, we will install lights—only if the standards can be disguised as trees." P. K. held firm until his 1977 death, by which time nearby residents had formed activist groups opposing lights as well. When the Tribune Company purchased the Cubs from the Wrigley family four years later, however, the issue came to a head. New general manager Dallas Green threatened that ownership would build a new park in the suburbs if residents didn't relent, and Major League Baseball discussed the possibility of moving any future Cubs home playoff games to Comiskey Park or St. Louis rather than lose the higher TV advertising revenue ensured by night contests.

Finally, on February 25, 1988, the Chicago City Council voted 29–19 to pass an ordinance permitting night games. Mayor Eugene Sawyer brokered a new deal with Cubs chairman John Madigan by which the team agreed to play eight night contests that season and 18 a year from 1989 through 2002 (plus any playoff or All-Star games). The antilight faction had a last laugh when the first after-dinner date with Philadelphia on August 8 (8/8/88) was called in the fourth inning due to torrential downpours, but the inevitable finally came to pass the next night: The crowd yelled "1-2-3. Let there be light!" Harry Grossman, a 91-year-old Cubs fan, flipped the switch, and Wrigley's streak of 6,852 straight day games was over. Oh yes, and Chicago beat the Mets 6–4.

Top: Along with the added TV and radio revenue generated from night games, Major League Baseball and the Tribune Company saw a great opportunity to reap even more financial benefits by marketing "Opening Night" as a historic event, with merchandise like this pennant selling well. *Bottom:* Here's one view that Goodyear blimp pilots probably thought they'd never see at night—Wrigley Field all aglow. Among its other benefits, the installation of lights at the ballpark allowed for prime-time TV coverage and overhead shots like this.

"Boys of Zimmer" Come Through

A managerial whipping boy in Boston for near-misses by the Red Sox, Don Zimmer became a cult hero as a Cubs skipper by leading a young club to a surprising NL East title in 1989. Part of his appeal was his take-no-guff approach with umpires, which he displays here to the delight of the Wrigley crowd.

There was so much hoopla surrounding the installation of lights at Wrigley Field during the 1988 season that many may have missed the promising happenings going on around the diamond. Although they won just one more game than the previous season (77–85), the Cubs moved up two notches in the standings to fourth place as several strong young players emerged. Greg Maddux, just 22, led the pitching staff with an 18–8 record, while left fielder Rafael Palmeiro (with a .307 average) and first baseman Mark Grace (.296), each playing his first full season, finished second and sixth respectively in the NL batting race.

New manager Don Zimmer, a seasoned skipper with a penchant for developing young talent, seemed a perfect choice to lead the team. Veterans Leon Durham, Jody Davis, and Keith Moreland departed the premises. By 1989, rookie outfielders Jerome Walton and Dwight Smith had also joined the mix, as well as young lefty reliever Mitch

Williams, picked up in a trade that sent Palmeiro to Texas. The young blood helped the Cubs move into first place by June, and after a slump dropped them briefly to third, they moved back on top with a terrific July and August— although the Cardinals and Mets were close behind right up until the final weeks.

"Old-timers" Ryne Sandberg (a team-high 30 homers), Andre Dawson (second with 21), and Rick Sutcliffe (16–11) remained on hand, but this title belonged to the kids. Maddux went 19–12 as the number one starter, and Williams had 36 saves out of the bullpen. Walton's 30-game hitting streak in July and August set a modern franchise record, and Smith hit .324. These performances, plus an expanded schedule of 18 night games, helped the Cubs set another team attendance record by drawing 2,491,942 fans, most of whom had high hopes that youth could be served in the playoffs.

He never matched his 16–1 Cy Young summer of 1984, but Rick Sutcliffe continued as one of Chicago's top starters (when healthy) during the years that followed. He led the NL with 18 wins in 1987, and he added 16 more in '89 to spark the Cubs to another NLCS berth.

IN 2003, RON SANTO BECAME
THE THIRD CUB TO HAVE HIS
NUMBER RETIRED, JOINING HALL
OF FAMERS ERNIE BANKS AND
BILLY WILLIAMS.

SEPTEMBER 28, 2003

Ron Santo
#10

CINCINNATI REDS at CHICAGO CUBS
WRIGLEY FIELD · CHICAGO, IL · JUNE 26, 2002

SAMMY
SOSA

AS THE
REIGNING MVP IN
THE MIDST OF ANOTHER
60-PLUS HOMER SEASON,
CUBS RIGHT FIELDER SAMMY SOSA
HAD PLENTY TO SMILE ABOUT IN 1999.

DESPITE A LINEUP WITH
SLUGGERS SAMMY
SOSA, FRED MCGRIFF,
AND MOISES ALOU,
MANAGER DON
BAYLOR'S CUBS LOST
THIS GAME 8-6.
SHORTLY THEREAFTER,
BAYLOR LOST HIS JOB.

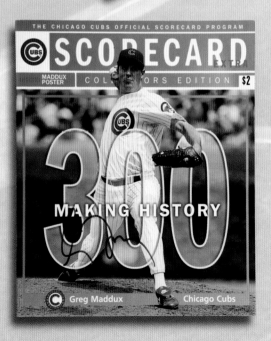

THE CHICAGO CUBS OFFICIAL SCORECARD PROGRAM
SCORECARD
EXTRA
MADDUX
POSTER
COLLECTORS EDITION
$2
300
MAKING HISTORY
Greg Maddux   Chicago Cubs

DON ZIMMER APPARENTLY
DIDN'T MIND COMPARISONS
WITH THE CARTOON SAILOR
TO WHICH MANY FELT THE
CUBS MANAGER BORE A
STRIKING RESEMBLANCE.

AFTER MADDUX RE-SIGNED WITH CHICAGO IN
2004, HE REMINDED CUBS FANS WHAT THEY HAD
BEEN MISSING FOR 11 YEARS BY GOING 16-11 AT
AGE 38. IN NOTCHING AN 8-4 VICTORY AT SAN
FRANCISCO ON AUGUST 7, HE BECAME THE 22ND
PITCHER IN ML HISTORY WITH 300 WINS.

AFTER AN ABRUPT RETIREMENT EARLY IN 1994, RYNE
SANDBERG RETURNED WITH POWER INTACT TO HIT
25 HOMERS AND DRIVE IN 92 RUNS IN '96.

Cubs rookie matches Rocket with 20-strikeout performance

CHICAGO, May 6, 1998—Making just his fifth major-league start, Cubs rookie Kerry Wood turned in one of the greatest pitching displays in baseball history today with a one-hit, 20-strikeout masterpiece over the Astros at rainy Wrigley Field.

The 2–0 victory, in which the 20-year-old fireballer yielded no walks and just a ground-ball single off third baseman Kevin Orie's glove in the third, tied him with Roger Clemens (who's done it twice) as the only pitchers to ever fan 20 in a nine-inning game. Wood, who twice hit 100 mph on the radar gun, whiffed eight of the last nine batters and had 15,758 fans standing and roaring throughout the ninth inning.

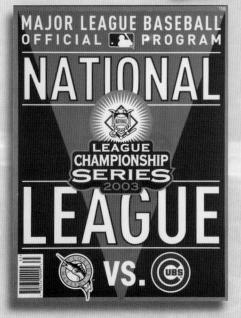

THOSE WHO BOUGHT
THIS PROGRAM AT
WRIGLEY FIELD FOR
GAMES 6 AND 7
SAW THE CUBS
COMPLETE ONE
OF THE GREATEST
POSTSEASON
COLLAPSES IN
HISTORY.

AFTER THE 2006 SEASON, A FAN
COULD SIT LIKE A BIG LEAGUER BY
PURCHASING THIS CHAIR FROM THE
CUBS CLUBHOUSE; NEW CHAIRS WERE
PURCHASED FOR THE LOCKER ROOM IN 2007.

Greg Maddux: The Right Stuff

The early 1990s did not provide much in the way of winning baseball at Wrigley Field, but at least Cubs fans were treated to a few more years watching one of the best young pitchers in the game: Greg Maddux.

Son of an Air Force officer-turned poker dealer, Maddux grew up in Las Vegas with his older brother, Mike (also a major-league pitcher). Both were drilled in baseball fundamentals by their father. Most scouts were initially put off by Greg's youthful appearance and slight 150-pound frame, but Doug Mapson of the Cubs believed Maddux had the poise and stuff to be a big winner.

On his advice, Chicago chose the high school senior in the second round of the 1984 draft, and Maddux was dispatched to Pikeville of the Appalachian League at age 18.

Maddux's ascent through the minor leagues was swift. After going 10–1 at Triple-A Iowa, the right-hander was called up by Chicago on September 1, 1986. He was still just 20 years old, the youngest Cub in two decades, but he managed to win twice in the season's waning weeks: a victory over the Reds (a complete game) and his brother Mike's Phillies (in the first-ever match-up of rookie brothers). The next season Greg took his lumps in the majors, making 27 starts for a sixth-place club and going 6–14 with a 5.61 ERA. Realizing that, even at a filled-out 170 pounds, he didn't have the size to be a true power pitcher, he

focused on gaining pinpoint control and an understanding of each hitter's tendencies. If he couldn't overpower them, he could certainly out-think them (and out-field them, as his 16 Gold Gloves attest).

Armed with this philosophy, Maddux began one of the most incredible stretches of consistency in baseball history starting in 1988. He won at least 15 games for a record *17 years in a row*. Unfortunately, only six of those seasons came in a Cubs uniform. After going 20–11 with a 2.18 ERA and 199 strikeouts to win the 1992 Cy Young Award, he signed with the Braves as a free agent and claimed the honor the next three years as well. When Maddux returned to the Cubs 12 years later, he was just in time to pick up his 300th career win.

Far left: After recording 18, 19, 15, and 15 victories the previous four seasons, control artist Greg Maddux finally joined the 20-win class in 1992. He was the first Cub to reach the mark since Rick Reuschel in '77. (Rick Sutcliffe's 20-win 1984 season included four wins with Cleveland.) *Left:* Here acknowledging a standing ovation at Wrigley Field after "K" No. 3,000, Maddux reached the hallowed mark in 2005 despite never leading his league in strikeouts. This was a testament to his incredible consistency; while flamethrowers such as Seaver, Ryan, and Clemens topped the charts with 250 or 300 whiffs, "Mad Dog" quietly notched his 180 to 199 year after year.

Sammy Sosa and the Home Run Chase

Prior to the 1998 season, Sammy Sosa was not a player whose name came up when people began speculating about who might be able to break Roger Maris's single-season home run record of 61. Cardinal first baseman Mark McGwire had crushed 58 long balls the previous summer, and Ken Griffey, Jr., of the Mariners, had poled 56. With 36 homers and a .251 batting average in '97, Sosa simply wasn't in their class.

Sammy, however, had spent the winter setting new goals with Cubs hitting coach Jeff Pentland, including swinging at fewer bad pitches and making contact with two strikes. He got off to a terrific start with a .333 batting average and 9 homers through May 24, but McGwire already had an incredible 24 homers. Nobody even mentioned their names in the same breath.

Then came June. Sosa had a record 20 homers during the month, and in one stretch slugged an incredible 17 in just 21 days. His streak thrust him into the national spotlight, and fans catching his act were delighted by his warm smile and touching gesture of tapping his fingers to his heart, kissing them, and pointing to the sky as he reached home plate on home-run trots. By the All-Star break, "Slammin' Sammy" had 33 and was just four behind "Big Mac." In mid-August, Sosa caught McGwire with his 47th round-tripper. By now the duo were a leading

news item nationwide, and at the start of September each had 55 blasts.

In the end, McGwire got to 62 first, hitting his milestone homer against the Cubs on September 8 as Sosa applauded and the Maris family watched. Once again Sosa hit two smashes to tie his rival, and in the last week of the season Sammy actually went ahead 66–65. But while Sosa was spent from the gripping pennant race, McGwire could focus on himself. He homered five times the final three games to beat Sosa 70 to 66, but there was no loser. Sosa would use his incredible MVP season (.308, 66 homers, 158 RBI) as a springboard to summers of 63, 50, and 64 homers the next three years. But thanks to the steroid scare, we're left to wonder just how "fair" a race Mac and Sammy really staged.

Left: Chicago and St. Louis were the places to be for baseball fans in 1998, as Sosa and McGwire both pursued the home run record of 61. When they met at Busch Stadium that season on August 7, Big Mac had 45 homers and Slammin' Sammy 43. One day later, both went deep again. *Above:* Sosa caught McGwire on September 13 with his 61st and (seen here) 62nd homers in an 11–10 victory over Milwaukee at Wrigley Field. McGwire had broken Maris's record with his 62nd amid great hoopla—and, interestingly, against the Cubs—five days before. Sammy had 58 then, but now Sosa had passed Roger, too. The race for a new mark was on.

"Kid K" and the Surprise Champs

As a young pitcher growing up in Texas, Kerry Wood followed the exploits of fellow natives Nolan Ryan and Roger Clemens. Once he made it to the majors in 1998, it didn't take the 20-year-old righty long to start achieving feats that even the two greatest strikeout artists in history could appreciate.

In addition to tying Clemens's record with 20 Ks in a nine-inning game, Wood had a 13–6 record and 233 total strikeouts over just $166^{2}/_{3}$ innings during his Rookie of the Year season. The performance capped a meteoric rise by the 6'5" youngster, who, after going 12–0 as a high school senior, had been Chicago's first selection (and the fourth pick overall) in the 1995 amateur draft. In his two full minor-league campaigns, he showed a "whiff" of what was to come with 329 strikeouts in $273^{1}/_{3}$ innings. When the Cubs

inexplicably sent him down to Triple-A Iowa to start the '98 season, Angels manager Terry Collins quipped: "If the Cubs have five pitchers better than Kerry Wood, they'll definitely win the World Series."

Collins's point, of course, was that the Cubs—coming off a dreadful 68–94, fifth-place season in 1997—possessed no such staff. What they did have, surprisingly, were enough terrific individual performances by Wood and others to put themselves into contention. Sammy Sosa rode the mother of all power grooves to a 66-homer, MVP season. Right-hander Kevin Tapani, hurt much of '97, rebounded to go 19–9. Henry Rodriguez, a newcomer playing left field, had 31 homers in just 415 at-bats. And Rod Beck had a team-record 51 saves out of the bullpen.

It all added up to a highly competitive club that, while unable to catch first-place Houston in the NL Central, did manage to tie San Francisco for the wild card spot when the Giants blew a 7–0 lead over Colorado on the season's final day. Kid K and Slammin' Sammy would have a crack at the playoffs, beginning with a one-game, winner-take-all battle with San Fran at Wrigley.

2003: Ecstasy and Agony

With the Cubs just one win away from their first World Series berth since 1945, the city of Chicago pulled out all the stops before Game 6 of the NLCS at Wrigley Field on October 14. As fans arrived at Wrigley for that night's game, these attractive banners greeted them outside the park.

S ammy Sosa provided a wonderful launching point for the 2003 season when he hit his 500th career home run off Scott Sullivan of the Reds April 4. Not to be outdone, Mark Prior and Kerry Wood both pitched stellar games the next few days. By the time Alex Gonzalez hit a walk-off homer to beat the Cardinals 3–2 at Wrigley Field on May 10, it appeared this was going to be a memorable year.

That it would be. The Cubs celebrated other milestones during the summer, including Sosa's 500th homer as a Cub and Wood's 1,000th strikeout, which came in just his 853rd inning— a new major-league record. A midseason slump briefly dropped the club to third place, but Chicago bounced back with a 19–8 September and clinched the NL Central crown with a doubleheader sweep of the Pirates at Wrigley on September 27.

The good feelings continued into the postseason, as the 88–74 Cubs upset the 101–61 Braves in a division series round that went the full five games and featured excellent starting performances from Prior and Wood. It marked the first playoff series the Cubs had won since the 1908 World Series, snapping a string of 10 consecutive postseason series setbacks spread over nearly 90 years. It appeared as if destiny might be playing a role in the season, especially when the Cubs took a 3-to-1 lead over the Florida Marlins in the

NLCS. As in 1984, they were just one game away from the World Series.

Florida's Josh Beckett pitched a 4–0 shut-out in Game 5, but Chicago still looked in fine shape when it took a 3–0 lead behind Prior into the eighth inning of the sixth contest. Then, with one out in the Marlin eighth and a man on second, Luis Castillo hit a foul ball toward the left-field stands. Moises Alou went to grab it, but a fan named Steve Bartman, who was tracking the ball instead of the fielder, seemed to knock it out of Alou's hands. Alou fumed, Castillo walked, and Florida quickly scored eight runs for the win. (Bartman needed a police escort to escape Wrigley Field.)

Once again, as in '84, everything came down to a final game. The Cubs rallied from a 3–0, first inning deficit to tie things on Wood's two-run homer, then they went ahead 5–3 on Alou's blast in the third. But Wood couldn't hold the lead, and when the bullpen failed as well, Florida captured the 9–6 victory and a date with the Yankees in the World Series.

There is perhaps no more despised photo in Chicago sports history than this one, which shows a true-blue Cubs fan (in cap and head-phones) forgetting Home Park Etiquette 101 as he appeared to prevent Moises Alou from catching a foul fly in Game 6. Until the Cubs win it all, this will remain the franchise's worst nightmare.

Making New History

CUBS

1908 · 2003

NEXT YEAR IS HERE!

BY JULY 2003, THE CUBS WERE LOOKING HOT WITH YOUNG ACES WOOD AND PRIOR IN THE ROTATION. AFTER REACHING THE NLCS, HOWEVER, THE TEAM FLAMED OUT.

BASEBALL MIDSEASON REPORT

MICHELLE WIE
Tiger Woman PAGE 37

Sports Illustrated

CHICAGO HEAT

Kerry Wood and Mark Prior Fire Up the Cubs

WHERE HAS THE BLACK BASEBALL PLAYER GONE? by Tom Verducci

SI's PLAYER SURVEY

Who They Like and Who They Don't
Umpires • Managers • Fans • Peers

RATHER THAN BE EMBARRASSED ABOUT THEIR TEAM'S FAILURE TO WIN A WORLD SERIES SINCE THE THEODORE ROOSEVELT ADMINISTRATION, CUBS FANS USE THE DUBIOUS HONOR AS A RALLYING CRY FOR THEIR CURRENT HEROES. THE 2003 TEAM DID INDEED MAKE HISTORY, BUT UNFORTUNATELY THE END RESULT WAS NOTHING NEW.

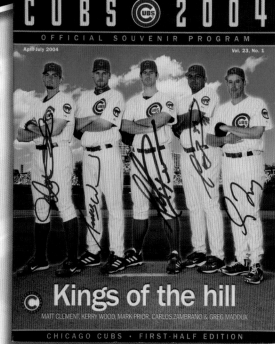

CUBS 2004

OFFICIAL SOUVENIR PROGRAM

April-July 2004   Vol. 23, No. 1

Kings of the hill

MATT CLEMENT, KERRY WOOD, MARK PRIOR, CARLOS ZAMBRANO & GREG MADDUX

CHICAGO CUBS · FIRST-HALF EDITION

CHICAGO'S 2004 ROTATION FEATURED VETERAN GREG MADDUX AND FOUR YOUNG FIREBALLERS. NOT SURPRISINGLY, CUBS PITCHERS LED THE NL WITH 1,346 STRIKEOUTS IN JUST 1,465⅓ INNINGS.

Braves sweep away Sosa, Cubs in NLDS

CHICAGO, Oct. 3, 1998—The Braves accomplished what few teams could this season, shutting down home run prince Sammy Sosa and completing a three-game sweep of the Cubs in the National League Division Series with a 6–2 victory at Wrigley Field tonight.

Getting terrific starting pitching for the third straight game—this time from ace Greg Maddux—the Braves led 1–0 before scoring five runs in the eighth off Chicago relievers Terry Mulholland and Rod Beck. Sosa, who hit 66 homers in the regular season, was not a factor. He went 0-for-4 today and 2-for-11 in the three games, with no RBI or runs scored.

THIS BALL SIGNED BY KERRY WOOD IS FROM THE 2003 ALL-STAR GAME, IN WHICH HE PITCHED ONE SCORELESS INNING. "KID K" LED THE NL WITH 266 STRIKEOUTS THAT SEASON.

THIS BATTING HELMET WAS AUTOGRAPHED BY MEMBERS OF THE 2007 CUBS AND IS A HANDSOME KEEPSAKE OF THE TEAM'S EXCITING "WORST TO FIRST" SEASON.

RYNE SANDBERG'S NO. 23 HAD ALREADY BEEN OUT OF CIRCULATION FOR EIGHT YEARS WHEN THE CUBS MADE ITS RETIREMENT OFFICIAL JUST AFTER RYNO'S HALL OF FAME INDUCTION.

Ryne Sandberg
#23
August 28, 2005
JERSEY RETIREMENT DAY

PEPSI
LOU PINIELLA

BOBBLEHEAD DOLLS HAVE BECOME A POPULAR SALES AND GIVEAWAY ITEM THROUGHOUT BASEBALL. THIS ONE HONORS CUBS MANAGER LOU PINIELLA OF THE 2007 NL CENTRAL CHAMPS.

SORIANO
12

ONE OF THE STARS BROUGHT IN BY MANAGEMENT FOR THE 2007 SEASON, ALFONSO SORIANO ROUTINELY GETS HIS UNIFORM DIRTY ON THE BASES AND IN THE OUTFIELD.

The State of Things Today

The best pure athlete on the 2007 Cubs may have been veteran Alfonso Soriano, who had 19 steals and 33 homers for the NL Central champs in his first season with the club. Once a second baseman with the Yankees, he developed into a top-notch left fielder who had 19 assists in '07.

T he Cubs are still hunting for their first World Series berth since 1945—and their first world championship in 100 years—but there is great reason to be optimistic about the current state of affairs at Wrigley Field. Under fiery new manager Lou Piniella, the 2007 club rebounded from a last-place finish the previous year and an 8½-game deficit in midseason to win the NL Central championship before being swept in the NL Division Series by Arizona.

A big factor in this turnaround was that the franchise made a financial commitment to winning. GM Jim Hendry spent $300 million to sign and re-sign big-name players prior to '07, and Piniella was willing to let rookies and younger players learn on the job. In new left fielder Alfonso Soriano and veterans Derrek Lee (at first base) and Aramis Ramirez (at third), Chicago had three terrific offensive players who provided 20- to 30-homer power to the lineup. Complementing these big bashers were scrappy youngsters such as second baseman Mike Fontenot, outfielder Matt Murton, and shortstop Ryan Theriot, the latter of whom led the club with 28 stolen bases. By the time he matures, young catcher Geovany Soto—who hit .389 in September after a monstrous .353 year with 26 homers and 109 RBI at Triple A—may be the best of them all.

While oft-injured former pitching ace Kerry Wood was relegated to bullpen duty during 2007, right-hander Carlos Zambrano (18–13) reigned as the rotation leader. Exciting on the mound and at the plate, he

Third baseman Aramis Ramirez, here notching a hit against the Giants in July, had his fourth straight outstanding season for the Cubs in 2007. He batted .310 with 26 home runs and 101 RBI and from 2004 to '07 averaged nearly 33 homers and 104 runs batted in per year.

was capable of striking out ten or smashing the ball out of the yard on any given day. He was complemented by a trio of fellow starters who all won in double figures: lefties Ted Lilly (15–8) and Rich Hill (11–8) and righty Jason Marquis (12–9). Closer Ryan Dempster contributed 28 saves, while fellow reliever Scott Eyre compiled a 0.81 ERA in the season's second half.

Then, of course, there is Piniella, who came to Chicago with more than 1,500 wins and a World Series championship (won with Cincinnati in 1990) on his managerial résumé. A two-time AL Manager of the Year winner, he turned a mediocre Mariners team into one of baseball's best and quickly announced his intentions to do the same in Chicago—then he delivered. "Long-suffering Cubs fans, we're going to win here," he said upon his hiring. "And that's really the end of the story."

It's also the end of this story. Cubs fans may indeed be long-suffering, but they are also supportive and confident—as the record

First baseman for the 2003 world champion Florida Marlins, Derrek Lee joined the Cubs the following season in a one-sided deal that only cost Chicago the underachieving Hee Seop Choi and career minor-leaguer Mike Nannini. Two years later Lee had a year for the ages with a .335 average, 46 homers, and 50 doubles. While he dipped in the ensuing seasons, he still contributed mightily.

crowds at Wrigley Field in 2007 attest. And as long as there is ivy on the walls of the building at the corner of Clark and Addison, they'll keep coming back for more.

The lights are on, the ticket prices have skyrocketed, but Wrigley Field is still the same ballpark where Cubs greats have shined since the days of Cy Williams and Hippo Vaughn. It's where Gabby beat the darkening skies, Lee and Borowy dazzled, Santo clicked his heels, Banks smashed No. 500, Fergie went the distance, Ryno showed his grit, Harry sang, and Sammy surpassed 60. It's home.

A Day at the Ballpark, 2007

Despite the familiar presence of the outfield ivy and a team unable to win (or even reach) a World Series, plenty has changed at Wrigley Field since the Tribune Corporation bought the Chicago Cubs in the early 1980s.

The fan-friendly team that once held back 23,000 unreserved seats for each home contest so folks could get seats on game days now sells all its tickets in advance—and the prices have skyrocketed. Fans of all persuasions attend games at Wrigley, but the underlying common factor is *money*. Many local kids can no longer afford to take the train down to the park and sit in the bleachers, which now cost $17 on special "value dates" and $42—yes, *$42* for seats without backs—on "special dates." Luxury boxes, built in 1988, cater to businesses, celebrities, and the rich, while even the "cheap" seats down the left- and right-field foul lines now cost more than box seats used to in the mid-1980s.

The food options have improved. Fresh pizza, pretzels, gourmet hot dogs, fries, and nachos are staples, along with different types of beer and soda depending on the fan's palate. In addition to the old reliable scorebook and pencil, there is more merchandise than ever before to choose from. A couple of the more intriguing items found in the ballpark's main souvenir store in recent years? A $250 Cubs leather jacket and a $20 Cubs Barbie doll (2003 prices).

The actual structure of Wrigley Field has not really changed much, which is just the way most fans like it. Folks arriving for this July 14, 2007, game against the Astros went past the same main marquee that has greeted patrons since the 1930s—although the electronic message board in its center has been added.

Only in the 1980s did the Cubs get serious about marketing, having largely resisted giveaway days (like Bat Day and Cap Day) that most teams had instituted back in the '70s. Now, however, fans coming to Wrigley almost always receive some sort of promotional item upon entering the park. Advertisers want very much to reach the baseball fan demographic, especially the 20- and 30-somethings hanging around Clark and Addison these days. If they can afford to attend baseball games, chances are they might be interested in a computer or car, too.

Then, of course, there are the lights. While Wrigley is still the ballpark most associated with day baseball (and bare-chested fans), some 25 home games a year now take place closer to suppertime than lunch. Some fans undoubtedly long for the old days—and no nights—but for the most part people have accepted the change. Although it needs a facelift now and then, Wrigley still charms Chicagoans as it nears its 100th birthday.

Wrigley "Bleacher Bums" once again had plenty to cheer about in 2007, although this picture would have looked much the same even if taken in the last-place season of '06. The fans have been packing the place to near capacity for a decade, and the Cubs set a new franchise attendance record of 3,252,462 in 2007.

CHAPTER EIGHT

LEADERS AND LEGENDS

Team History

Nicknames

White Stockings (1876–89)
Black Stockings (1888–89)
Colts (1890–97)
Ex-Colts (1898)
Rainmakers (1898)
Orphans (1898–1902)
Cowboys (1899)
Rough Riders (1899–1900)
Remnants (1901–02)
Cubs (1902–Present)
Recruits (1902)
Panamas (1903)
Zephyrs (1905)
Nationals (1905–07)
Spuds (1906)
Trojans (1913)

World Series

1907, 1908

Pennant Winners

1876, 1880, 1881, 1882, 1885,
1886, 1906, 1907, 1908, 1910,
1918, 1929, 1932, 1935, 1938,
1945

Division Winners

1984, National League East
1989, National League East
2003, National League Central
2007, National League Central

Playoff Wild Card Clubs

1998, National League Central

Ballparks

23rd Street Grounds (1876–77)
Lakefront Park (1878–84)
West Side Park (1885–91)
South Side Park (1891–93)
West Side Grounds (1893–1915)
Weeghman Park/Wrigley Field
    (1916–Present)

Game-worn Cubs away helmet

Hall of Fame Members

(by primary position; years with Cubs indicated)

Grover Alexander, P, 1918–26
Mordecai Brown, P, 1904–12,
    1916 *
John Clarkson, P, 1884–87
Dizzy Dean, P, 1938–41
Dennis Eckersley, P, 1984–86
Clark Griffith, P, 1893–1900
    (inducted as manager)
Burleigh Grimes, P, 1932–33
Fergie Jenkins, P, 1966–73,
    1982–83 *
Robin Roberts, P, 1966
Albert Spalding, P, 1876–78
Bruce Sutter, P, 1976–80
Rube Waddell, P, 1901
Hoyt Wilhelm, P, 1970
Roger Bresnahan, C, 1900,
    1913–15
Gabby Hartnett, C, 1922–40 *
Cap Anson, 1B, 1876–97 *
Frank Chance, 1B, 1898–1912 *
Jimmie Foxx, 1B, 1942, 1944

George Kelly, 1B, 1930
Johnny Evers, 2B, 1902–13 *
Billy Herman, 2B, 1931–41 *
Rogers Hornsby, 2B, 1929–32
Tony Lazzeri, 2B, 1938
Ryne Sandberg, 2B, 1982–94;
    1996–97 *
Ernie Banks, SS, 1953–71 *
Rabbit Maranville, SS, 1925
Joe Tinker, SS, 1902–12, 1916 *
Fred Lindstrom, 3B, 1935
Lou Brock, LF, 1961–64
Monte Irvin, LF, 1956
Ralph Kiner, LF, 1953–54
Billy Williams, LF, 1959–74 *
Richie Ashburn, CF, 1960–61
Hugh Duffy, CF, 1888–89
Hack Wilson, CF, 1926–31 *
Kiki Cuyler, RF, 1928–35
King Kelly, RF, 1880–86 *
Chuck Klein, RF, 1934–36
* Entered Hall of Fame as Cub

Non-players

Lou Boudreau, manager,
    1960 (inducted as shortstop)
Leo Durocher, manager, 1966–72

Frankie Frisch, manager,
    1949–51 (inducted as second
    baseman)
Joe McCarthy, manager, 1926–30
Frank Selee, manager, 1902–05
William Hulbert, executive,
    1876–82

Broadcasters (years with Cubs)

Jack Brickhouse, 1941–45,
    1947–81
Harry Caray, 1982–97
Jimmy Dudley, 1941–42
Bob Elson, 1929–41
Milo Hamilton, 1955–57,
    1980–84
Russ Hodges, 1935–37

Retired Uniform Numbers

Ernie Banks - 14
Jackie Robinson - 42 *
Ryne Sandberg - 23
Ron Santo - 10
Billy Williams - 26
* Retired by all major-league clubs

Our Picks: All-Time Cubs

All-Time Cubs All-Star Team
C Gabby Hartnett

Ryne Sandberg entered the Hall of Fame in 2005.

1B Cap Anson
2B Ryne Sandberg
SS Ernie Banks
3B Ron Santo
LF Billy Williams
CF Hack Wilson
RF Sammy Sosa
RHSP Mordecai Brown
LHSP Hippo Vaughn
RP Bruce Sutter

The Second Team:
C Johnny Kling
1B Frank Chance
2B Billy Herman
SS Bill Dahlen
3B Stan Hack
LF Hank Sauer
CF Jimmy Ryan
RF Kiki Cuyler
RHSP Fergie Jenkins
LHSP Jack Pfiester
RP Lee Smith

Top five catchers:
Gabby Hartnett
Johnny Kling
Randy Hundley

Jody Davis
Jimmy Archer

Top five first basemen:
Cap Anson
Frank Chance
Mark Grace
Phil Cavarretta
Charlie Grimm

Top five second basemen:
Ryne Sandberg
Billy Herman
Johnny Evers
Rogers Hornsby
Fred Pfeffer

Top five shortstops:
Ernie Banks
Bill Dahlen
Woody English
Joe Tinker
Billy Jurges

Top five third basemen:
Ron Santo
Stan Hack
Aramis Ramirez
Ned Williamson
Heinie Zimmerman

Top five left fielders:
Billy Williams
Hank Sauer
Riggs Stephenson
Abner Dalrymple
Jimmy Sheckard

Top five center fielders:
Hack Wilson
Jimmy Ryan
George Gore
Rick Monday
Andy Pafko

Top five right fielders:
Sammy Sosa
Kiki Cuyler
Bill Nicholson
King Kelly
Andre Dawson

Top ten right-handed starters:
Mordecai Brown
Fergie Jenkins
Grover Alexander
Clark Griffith
Larry Corcoran
Ed Reulbach
Charlie Root
Rick Reuschel
Greg Maddux
Claude Passeau

Top five left-handed starters:
Hippo Vaughn
Jack Pfiester
Ken Holtzman
Larry French
Dick Ellsworth

Top five relievers:
Bruce Sutter
Lee Smith

Randy Myers

Phil Regan

Lindy McDaniel

Award Winners

Most Valuable Player

Frank Schulte (Chalmers Award), RF, 1911

Rogers Hornsby (League), 2B, 1929

Gabby Hartnett, C, 1935

Phil Cavarretta, 1B, 1945

Hank Sauer, LF, 1952

Ernie Banks, SS, 1958

Ernie Banks, SS, 1959

Ryne Sandberg, 2B, 1984

Andre Dawson, RF, 1987

Sammy Sosa, RF, 1998

Cy Young Award

Fergie Jenkins, 1971

Bruce Sutter, 1979

Rick Sutcliffe, 1984

Greg Maddux, 1992

Rookie of the Year

Billy Williams, LF, 1961

Ken Hubbs, 2B, 1962

Jerome Walton, CF, 1989

Kerry Wood, P, 1998

Gold Glove

Ernie Banks, SS, 1960

Ken Hubbs, 2B, 1962

Ron Santo, 3B, 1964, 1965, 1966, 1967, 1968

Randy Hundley, C, 1967

Glenn Beckert, 2B, 1968

Don Kessinger, SS, 1969, 1970

Ryne Sandberg, 2B, 1983, 1984, 1985, 1986, 1987, 1988, 1989, 1990, 1991

Bob Dernier, CF, 1984

Jody Davis, C, 1986

Andre Dawson, RF, 1987, 1988

Greg Maddux, P, 1990, 1991, 1992

Mark Grace, 1B, 1992, 1993, 1995, 1996

Derrek Lee, 1B, 2005, 2007

All-Star Game MVP

Bill Madlock, 3B, 1975

Batting Records

National League Leaders
(* = tied)

Batting

Ross Barnes, 1876 - .429

George Gore, 1880 - .360

Cap Anson, 1881 - .399

King Kelly, 1884 - .354

King Kelly, 1886 - .388

Cap Anson, 1888 - .344

Heinie Zimmerman, 1912 - .372

Phil Cavarretta, 1945 - .355

Billy Williams, 1972 - .333

Bill Madlock, 1975 - .354

Bill Madlock, 1976 - .339

Bill Buckner, 1980 - .324

Runs Scored

Ross Barnes, 1876 - 126

Abner Dalrymple, 1880 - 91

George Gore, 1881 - 86

George Gore, 1882 - 99

King Kelly, 1884 - 120

King Kelly, 1885 - 124

King Kelly, 1886 - 155

Frank Chance, 1906 - 103 *

Jimmy Sheckard, 1911 - 121

Tommy Leach, 1913 - 99

Rogers Hornsby, 1929 - 156

Augie Galan, 1935 - 133

Bill Nicholson, 1944 - 116

Glenn Beckert, 1968 - 98

Billy Williams, 1970 - 137

Ivan DeJesus, 1978 - 104

Ryne Sandberg, 1984 - 114

Ryne Sandberg, 1989 - 104 *

Ryne Sandberg, 1990 - 116

Sammy Sosa, 1998 - 134

Sammy Sosa, 2001 - 146

Sammy Sosa, 2002 - 122

Hits

Ross Barnes, 1876 - 138

Joe Start, 1878 - 100

Abner Dalrymple, 1880 - 126

Cap Anson, 1881 - 137

Jimmy Ryan, 1888 - 182

Harry Steinfeldt, 1906 - 176

Heinie Zimmerman, 1912 - 207

Charlie Hollocher, 1918 - 161

Billy Herman, 1935 - 227

Stan Hack, 1940 - 191 *

Stan Hack, 1941 - 186

Phil Cavarretta, 1944 - 197 *

Billy Williams, 1970 - 205 *

Derrek Lee, 2005 - 199

Juan Pierre, 2006 - 204

Doubles

Ross Barnes, Paul Hines, 1876 - 21 *

Cap Anson, 1877 - 19

King Kelly, 1881 - 27 *

King Kelly, 1882 - 37

Ned Williamson, 1883 - 49

Cap Anson, 1885 - 35

Jimmy Ryan, 1888 - 33

Heinie Zimmerman, 1912 - 41

Riggs Stephenson, 1927 - 46

Kiki Cuyler, 1934 - 42

Billy Herman, 1935 - 57

Bill Buckner, 1981 - 35

Bill Buckner, 1983 - 38 *

Mark Grace, 1995 - 51

Triples

Ross Barnes, 1876 - 14

Frank Schulte, 1906 - 13 *

Vic Saier, 1913 - 21

Billy Herman, 1939 - 18

George Altman, 1961 - 12

Ron Santo, 1964 - 13 *

Ryne Sandberg, 1984 - 19 *

Home Runs

Ned Williamson, 1884 - 27

Abner Dalrymple, 1885 - 11

Jimmy Ryan, 1888 - 16

Walt Wilmot, 1890 - 13 *

Kerry Wood will go in the record books as a pitcher, but he does have seven home runs to his credit.

Frank Schulte, 1910 - 10 *
Frank Schulte, 1911 - 21
Heinie Zimmerman, 1912 - 14
Cy Williams, 1916 - 12 *
Hack Wilson, 1926 - 21
Hack Wilson, 1927 - 30 *
Hack Wilson, 1928 - 31 *
Hack Wilson, 1930 - 56
Bill Nicholson, 1943 - 29
Bill Nicholson, 1944 - 33
Hank Sauer, 1952 - 37 *
Ernie Banks, 1958 - 47
Ernie Banks, 1960 - 41
Dave Kingman, 1979 - 48
Andre Dawson, 1987 - 49
Ryne Sandberg, 1990 - 40
Sammy Sosa, 2000 - 50
Sammy Sosa, 2002 - 49

Runs Batted In (RBI)

Deacon White, 1876 - 60
Cap Anson, 1880 - 74
Cap Anson, 1881 - 82
Cap Anson, 1882 - 83
Cap Anson, 1884 - 102
Cap Anson, 1885 - 108
Cap Anson, 1886 - 147
Cap Anson, 1888 - 84
Cap Anson, 1891 - 120
Harry Steinfeldt, 1906 - 83 *
Frank Schulte, 1911 - 107 *
Hack Wilson, 1929 - 159
Hack Wilson, 1930 - 191
Bill Nicholson, 1943 - 128
Bill Nicholson, 1944 - 122
Hank Sauer, 1952 - 121
Ernie Banks, 1958 - 129

Ernie Banks, 1959 - 143
Andre Dawson, 1987 - 137
Sammy Sosa, 1998 - 158
Sammy Sosa, 2001 - 160

Stolen Bases

Bill Lange, 1897 - 73
Frank Chance, 1903 - 67 *
Bill Maloney, 1905 - 59 *
Frank Chance, 1906 - 57
Kiki Cuyler, 1928 - 37
Kiki Cuyler, 1929 - 43
Kiki Cuyler, 1930 - 37
Augie Galan, 1935 - 22
Augie Galan, 1937 - 23
Stan Hack, 1938 - 16
Stan Hack, 1939 - 17 *

Career Team Batting Leaders (Top Ten)
Games

Ernie Banks - 2,528
Cap Anson - 2,276
Billy Williams - 2,213
Ryne Sandberg - 2,151
Ron Santo - 2,126
Phil Cavarretta - 1,953
Stan Hack - 1,938
Gabby Hartnett - 1,926
Mark Grace - 1,910
Sammy Sosa - 1,811

Average (minimum 1,450 at-bats)

Riggs Stephenson - .336
Bill Madlock - .336
Bill Lange - .330
Cap Anson - .329

Kiki Cuyler - .325
Bill Everitt - .323
Hack Wilson - .322
King Kelly - .316
George Gore - .315
Frank Demaree - .309
Billy Herman - .309

Runs Scored

Cap Anson - 1,719
Jimmy Ryan - 1,409
Ryne Sandberg - 1,316
Billy Williams - 1,306
Ernie Banks - 1,305
Sammy Sosa - 1,245
Stan Hack - 1,239
Ron Santo - 1,109
Mark Grace - 1,057
Phil Cavarretta - 968

Hits

Cap Anson - 2,995
Ernie Banks - 2,583
Billy Williams - 2,510
Ryne Sandberg - 2,385
Mark Grace - 2,201
Stan Hack - 2,193
Ron Santo - 2,171
Jimmy Ryan - 2,073
Sammy Sosa - 1,985
Phil Cavarretta - 1,927

Doubles

Cap Anson - 528
Mark Grace - 456
Ernie Banks - 407
Ryne Sandberg - 403
Billy Williams - 402

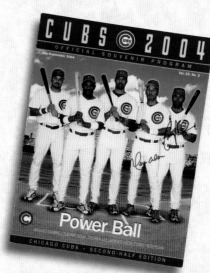

Power hitters Aramis Ramirez, Sammy Sosa, Derrek Lee, Moises Alou, and Corey Patterson are pictured on this program.

Gabby Hartnett - 391
Stan Hack - 363
Jimmy Ryan - 362
Ron Santo - 353
Billy Herman - 346

Triples

Jimmy Ryan - 142
Cap Anson - 124
Frank Schulte - 117
Bill Dahlen - 106
Phil Cavarretta - 99
Joe Tinker - 93
Ernie Banks - 90
Billy Williams - 87
Stan Hack - 81

Home Runs

Sammy Sosa - 545
Ernie Banks - 512
Billy Williams - 392
Ron Santo - 337

Ryne Sandberg - 282
Gabby Hartnett - 231
Bill Nicholson - 205
Hank Sauer - 198
Hack Wilson - 190
Andre Dawson - 174

Runs Batted In
Cap Anson - 1,879
Ernie Banks - 1,636
Sammy Sosa - 1,414
Billy Williams - 1,353
Ron Santo - 1,290
Gabby Hartnett - 1,153
Ryne Sandberg - 1,061
Mark Grace - 1,004
Jimmy Ryan - 914
Phil Cavarretta - 896

Slugging Percentage
Hack Wilson - .590
Sammy Sosa - .569
Hank Sauer - .512
Andre Dawson - .507
Billy Williams - .503
Derrek Lee - .502
Ernie Banks - .500
Aramis Ramirez - .500
Gabby Hartnett - .490
Kiki Cuyler - .485
Leon Durham - .484
Ron Santo - .472

Stolen Bases
Frank Chance - 400
Bill Lange - 399
Jimmy Ryan - 369
Ryne Sandberg - 344

Joe Tinker - 304
Johnny Evers - 291
Walt Wilmot - 290
Bill Dahlen - 285
Fred Pfeffer - 263
Cap Anson - 247

Other Batting Feats
Most Home Runs at Wrigley Field
Sammy Sosa - 293
Ernie Banks - 290
Billy Williams - 231
Ron Santo - 212
Ryne Sandberg - 164

Pitching Records

National League Leaders
(= tie)*

Victories
Al Spalding, 1876 - 47
Larry Corcoran, 1881 - 31
John Clarkson, 1885 - 53
John Clarkson, 1887 - 38
Bill Hutchison, 1890 - 41
Bill Hutchison, 1891 - 44
Bill Hutchison, 1892 - 36
Mordecai Brown, 1909 - 27
Larry Cheney, 1912 - 26 *
Hippo Vaughn, 1918 - 22
Grover Alexander, 1920 - 27
Charlie Root, 1927 - 26
Pat Malone, 1929 - 22
Pat Malone, 1930 - 20

Lon Warneke, 1932 - 22
Bill Lee, 1938 - 22
Larry Jackson, 1964 - 24
Fergie Jenkins, 1971 - 24
Rick Sutcliffe, 1987 - 18
Greg Maddux, 1992 - 20 *
Carlos Zambrano, 2006 - 16 *

Earned-Run Average (ERA)
Larry Corcoran, 1882 - 1.95
Clark Griffith, 1898 - 1.88
Jack Taylor, 1902 - 1.33
Mordecai Brown, 1906 - 1.04
Jack Pfiester, 1907 - 1.15
Hippo Vaughn, 1918 - 1.74
Grover Alexander, 1919 - 1.72
Grover Alexander, 1920 - 1.91
Lon Warneke, 1932 - 2.37
Bill Lee, 1938 - 2.66
Hank Borowy, 1945 - 2.13

Strikeouts
Larry Corcoran, 1880 - 268
John Clarkson, 1885 - 308
John Clarkson, 1887 - 237
Bill Hutchison, 1892 - 314
Orval Overall, 1909 - 205
Hippo Vaughn, 1918 - 148
Hippo Vaughn, 1919 - 141
Grover Alexander, 1920 - 173
Pat Malone, 1929 - 166
Clay Bryant, 1938 - 135
Johnny Schmitz, 1946 - 135
Sam Jones, 1955 - 198
Sam Jones, 1956 - 176

Fergie Jenkins, 1969 - 273
Kerry Wood, 2003 - 266

Innings Pitched
John Clarkson, 1885 - 623.0
Bill Hutchison, 1890 - 603.0
Bill Hutchison, 1891 - 561.0
Bill Hutchison, 1892 - 622.0
Mordecai Brown, 1909 - 342.2
Hippo Vaughn, 1918 - 290.1
Hippo Vaughn, 1919 - 306.2
Grover Alexander, 1920 - 363.1
Charlie Root, 1927 - 309.0
Fergie Jenkins, 1971 - 325.0
Greg Maddux, 1991 - 263.0
Greg Maddux, 1992 - 268.0
Jon Lieber, 2000 - 251.0

Complete Games
John Clarkson, 1885 - 68
John Clarkson, 1887 - 56
Bill Hutchison, 1890 - 65
Bill Hutchison, 1891 - 56
Bill Hutchison, 1892 - 67
Clark Griffith, 1897 - 38 *

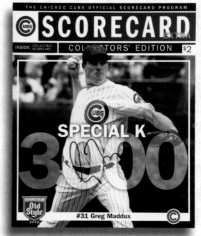

Maddux got his 3,000th strikeout at Wrigley Field on July 26, 2005.

Mordecai Brown, 1909 - 32
Mordecai Brown, 1910 - 27
Larry Cheney, 1912 - 28
Grover Alexander, 1920 - 33
Pat Malone, 1930 - 22 *
Lon Warneke, 1933 - 26 *
Fergie Jenkins, 1967 - 20
Fergie Jenkins, 1970 - 24
Fergie Jenkins, 1971 - 30

Saves (since 1960)

Lindy McDaniel, 1963 - 22
Ted Abernathy, 1965 - 31
Phil Regan, 1968 - 25
Bruce Sutter, 1979 - 37
Bruce Sutter, 1980 - 28
Lee Smith, 1983 - 29
Randy Myers, 1993 - 53
Randy Myers, 1995 - 38

All-Time Team Pitching Leaders
Victories

Charlie Root - 201
Mordecai Brown - 188
Bill Hutchison - 181
Larry Corcoran - 175
Fergie Jenkins - 167
Clark Griffith - 152
Guy Bush - 152
Hippo Vaughn - 151
Bill Lee - 139
John Clarkson - 137

Strikeouts

Fergie Jenkins - 2,038
Charlie Root - 1,432
Rick Reuschel - 1,367

Kerry Wood - 1,323
Greg Maddux - 1,305
Bill Hutchison - 1,224
Hippo Vaughn - 1,138
Larry Corcoran - 1,086
Bob Rush - 1,076
Mordecai Brown - 1,043

Earned-Run Average (minimum 1,000 innings)

Mordecai Brown - 1.80
Jack Pfiester - 1.85
Orval Overall - 1.91
Ed Reulbach - 2.24
Larry Corcoran - 2.26
Hippo Vaughn - 2.33
Terry Larkin - 2.34
John Clarkson - 2.39
Carl Lundgren - 2.42
Jack Taylor - 2.66

Shutouts (since 1900)

Mordecai Brown - 48
Hippo Vaughn - 35
Ed Reulbach - 31
Fergie Jenkins - 29
Orval Overall - 28
Bill Lee - 25
Grover Alexander - 24
Claude Passeau - 22
Larry French - 21
Charlie Root - 21

Saves (since 1960)

Lee Smith - 180
Bruce Sutter - 133
Randy Myers - 112

Ryan Dempster - 87
Phil Regan - 60
Rod Beck - 58
Mitch Williams - 52
Joe Borowski - 44
Ted Abernathy - 39
Lindy McDaniel - 39

Innings Pitched

Charlie Root - 3,137.1
Bill Hutchison - 3,021.0
Fergie Jenkins - 2,673.2
Larry Corcoran - 2,338.1
Mordecai Brown - 2,329.0
Rick Reuschel - 2,290.0
Bill Lee - 2,271.1
Hippo Vaughn - 2,216.1
Clark Griffith - 2,188.2
Guy Bush - 2,101.2

No-Hit Games

Larry Corcoran vs. Boston,
    August 19, 1880, 6–0
Larry Corcoran vs. Worcester,
    September 20, 1882, 5–0
Larry Corcoran vs. Providence,
    June 27, 1884, 6–0
John Clarkson at Providence,
    July 27, 1885, 4–0
George van Haltren vs.
    Pittsburgh, June 21, 1888,
    1–0 (6)
Walter Thornton vs. Brooklyn,
    August 21, 1898, 2–0
Bob Wicker at New York,
    June 11, 1904, 1–0 (12)
Allowed only hit after 9.1 hitless
    innings

Jody Davis earned a Gold Glove
Award in 1986.

King Cole at St. Louis,
    July 31, 1910, 4–0 (7)
Jimmy Lavender at New York,
    August 31, 1915, 2–0
Hippo Vaughn vs. Cincinnati,
    May 2, 1917, 0–1 (10)
Allowed first hit after 9.1 hitless
    innings; allowed 2 more hits
    in 10th for loss; Fred Toney of
    Cincinnati pitched 10-inning
    no-hitter for the win
Sam Jones vs. Pittsburgh,
    May 12, 1955, 4–0
Don Cardwell vs. St. Louis,
    May 15, 1960, 4–0
Ken Holtzman vs. Atlanta,
    August 19, 1969, 3–0
Ken Holtzman at Cincinnati,
    June 3, 1971, 1–0
Only night no-hitter by a Cub
Burt Hooton vs. Philadelphia
    April 16, 1972 , 4–0
Milt Pappas vs. San Diego,
    September 2, 1972, 8–0
Pappas lost a perfect game on walk
    with two outs in ninth

Index